DESIGN

by **MILTON GLASER** and **MIRKO ILIĆ**

DSSENT

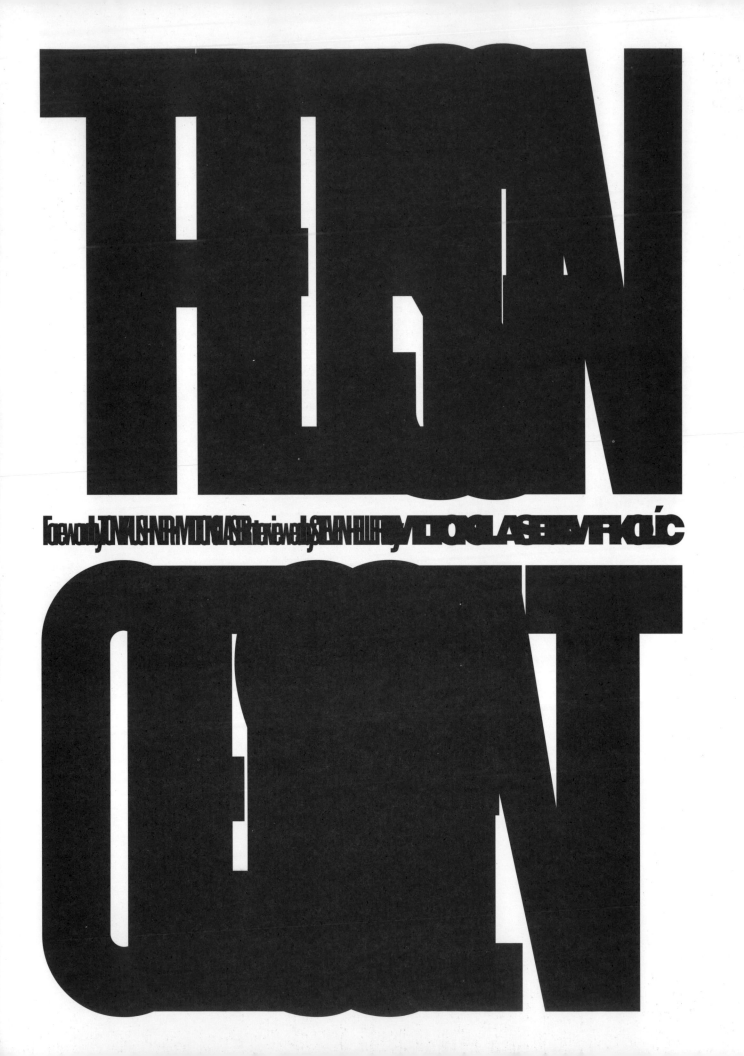

Foreword by JONAS HNER M DOUGLAS R, reviewed by STEVAN HELLER by VJEKOSLAV SEBE M FRKOLIĆ

Title: Let My People Go
Format: Poster
Art Director/Designer:
Dan Reisinger
Client: No client
Country: Israel
Year: 1969

By adapting the communist hammer and sickle, this poster opposes the Soviet policy prohibiting the immigration of Jews from the USSR. (top left)

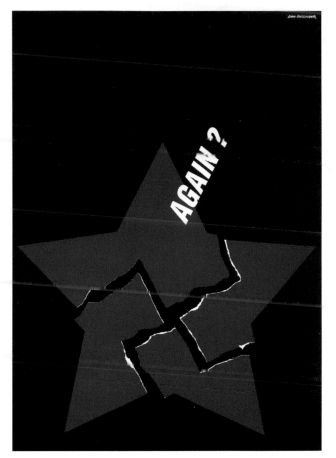

Title: Again?
Format: Poster
Art Director/Designer:
Dan Reisinger
Client: No client
Country: Israel
Year: 1993

A prescient 1993 warning against the resurgence of fascistic and anti-Semitic movements in the formerly communist countries of Eastern Europe is the message of this bold and dynamic poster. (top right)

Title: Diskurs Macht hegemonie
Format: Magazine cover
Art Director/Designer:
Rico Lins
Client: Germinal Verlag, Bochum/Klartext Verlag, Bochum
Country: Brazil
Year: 1988

This image for the German political magazine *KulturRevolution* is a collaged composite, a Mr. Potato Head, if you will, of four left-wing icons, Mao Tse Tung, Karl Marx, Leon Trotsky, and Michel Foucault, symbolizing an attempt to combine various ideologies in hopes of creating something stronger, when, in fact, the result does not work. (bottom)

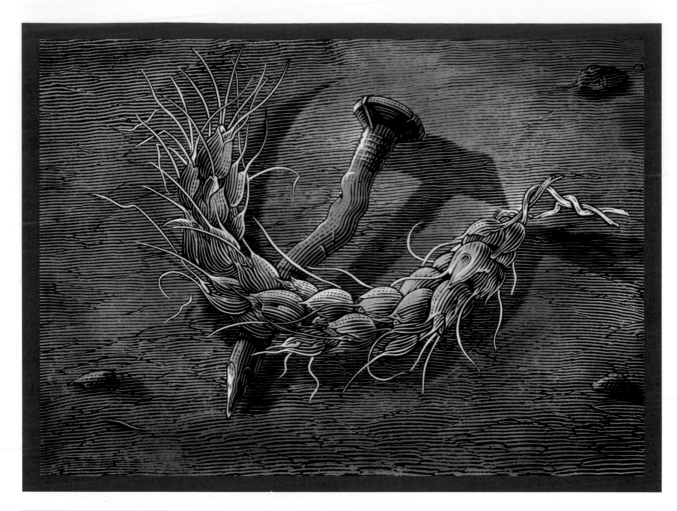

Title: **Nail and Wheat**
Format: **Poster**
Art Director/Designer:
Istvan Orosz
Client: **No client**
Country: **Hungary**
Year: **1989**

The careful placement of the nail (hit with the hammer) and sheath of wheat (cut with the sickle) in the position of the Soviet hammer and sickle symbol convey the victimization of people under communism.

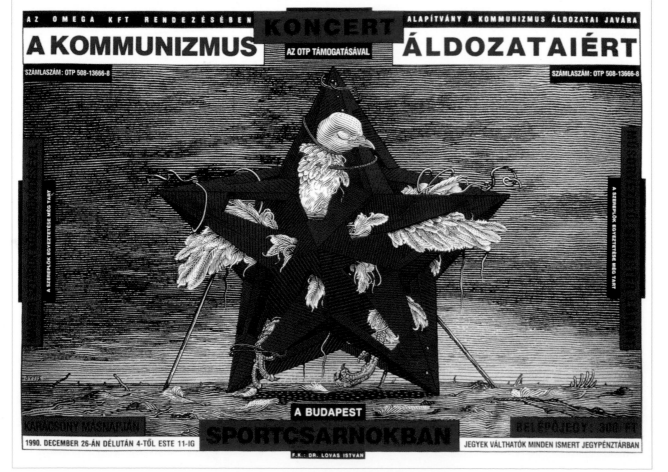

Title: **Concert Poster**
Format: **Poster**
Art Director/Designer:
Istvan Orosz
Client: **No client**
Country: **Hungary**
Year: **1990**

This bold and immediate poster advertises a Budapest concert for the victims of communism.

Title: **Comrades, It's Over**
Format: **Poster**
Art Director/Designer:
Istvan Orosz
Client: **M.D.F.**
Country: **Hungary**
Year: **1989**

This work was created by a designer/illustrator who grew up in, and spent his life in, Soviet-dominated Hungary. He was surprised and delighted in 1989 when he drew this poster and soon afterward, the Soviet Army returned home.

Title: **Poster to Commemorate the Day of Yugoslav Youth**
Format: **Poster**
Art Director/Designer: **New Collectivism**
Client: **Socialist Youth League of Slovenia**
Country: **Slovenia**
Year: **1987**

This prize-winning poster celebrating Marshall Josip Broz Tito's birthday is a redesign of a 1930's Richard Klein poster (*below*). NSK (Neue Slowenische Kunst) believes the traumas of the past affecting the present and the future can be healed only by returning to the initial conflicts. NSK narrowly escaped imprisonment when the original Nazi source became public knowledge.

aTitle: **Exterior of the NSK State Berlin**
Format: **Exterior design**
Art Director/Designer: **New Collectivism**
Client: **Volksbuhne Theater**
Country: **Slovenia**
Year: **1993**

NSK hosted a show at the Volksbuhne theater in the historical center of Berlin, once among the most prominent theater establishments of the twentieth century. During the show, the Volksbuhne was declared a territory of the NSK State and entry was only permitted to NSK passport holders with valid visas. However, a "consulate office" was open non-stop issuing information and documents to potential NSK citizens interested in entering. (*top*)

Title: **NSK Headquarters**
Format: **Photograph**
Art Director/Designer: **New Collectivism**
Client: **NSK Information Center**
Country: **Slovenia**
Year: **1999**

Shown here is the NSK state information office. The passport division is placed in front of a wall mounted with photographs of various NSK artifacts. (*bottom left*)

Title: **The State of NSK**
Format: **Poster**
Art Director/Designer: **New Collectivism**
Client: **NSK**
Country: **Slovenia**
Year: **1994**

New Collectivism is an independent graphic design collective and a member of the NSK organization. In this poster, the Utopian goal is expressed by NSK as a state. This poster was used to promote various NSK events. (*bottom right*)

NSK TRGOVINA

MANJ JE VEČ, PA ŠE VEDNO NE DOVOLJ

NSK MERCHANDISE
NSK Info Center
p.p. 101, SI-1001 Ljubljana
Slovenia, NSK

PLOŠČE/RECORDS
kos/piece **2.499,-**

VIDEOKASETE/VIDEOTAPES
kos/piece **4.999,-**

PLAKATI/POSTERS
999,- kos/piece

MAJICE SHIRTS
2.899,-

NOORDUNG KOLEDAR
3.999,-
NOORDUNG CALENDAR

SPOMINSKI KROŽNIKI MEMORIAL PLATES
Oblikovanje/Design by:
Charlie Krafft
NOVO
kos/piece **2.999,-**

NALEPKA/STICKER
NATO LAIBACH NSK
kos/piece **299,-**

KNJIGE ODDELKA ZA ČISTO IN PRAKTIČNO FILOZOFIJO PRI NSK BOOKS OF THE DEPARTMENT OF PURE AND APPLIED PHILOSOPHY AT NSK
2.999,- kos/piece

NSK POST/NSK POŠTA
499,-

KRAVATA TIE
3.899,-

IGLA ZA KRAVATO/TIE-PIN
1.499,-

ZNAČKA/BADGE
999,-

ŠAL/SCARF
3.899,-

SKODELICA IN PODSTAVEK CUP AND SAUCER
2.499,-

MEDVEDKA/SHE BEAR
Oblikovanje/Design by: Irwin
29.899,-

POŠTNE RAZGLEDNICE POSTCARDS
4.999,-

NSK KNJIGA/NSK BOOK
2.999,-

Title: **NSK Merchandise**
Format: **Book cover**
Art Director/Designer:
New Collectivism
Client: **No client**
Country: **Slovenia**
Year: **1999**

The back cover of the NSK catalog/monograph shows NSK merchandise designed for an exhibition at the Museum of Modern Art in Ljubljana. The transition from socialism to capitalism and the creation of European monetary union in 1999 is represented by the number 99 shown throughout. All products featured are for sale.

Title: **What, how & for whom–152nd anniversary of the Communist Manifesto**
Format: **Book/Catalogue**
Art Director/Designer: **Dejan Kršić**
Client: **What, how & for whom (WHW)**
Country: **Croatia**
Year: **2003**

The dynamic cover of this 152nd Anniversary edition of the *The Communist Manifesto* boldly features Karl Marx and Friedrich Engles. The book serves as a catalog to an exhibition and various events held in Croatia that were re-staged the following year in Austria. The publication contains essays by several famous theoreticians and writers, and is distributed in bookshops, galleries, and museums.

1er EXPO en FRANCE de PÉTER PÓCS
MAIRIE DE CASTELMORON DU 8 AU 28 AOUT TOUS LES APRÉS-MIDI

L'AFFICHE A CASTELMORON D'ALBRETE

Title: **Péter Pócs's First Exhibition in France**
Format: **Poster**
Art Director/Designer: **Péter Pócs**
Client: **Unknown**
Country: **Hungary**
Year: **1988**

This poster was originally designed for an exhibition of Hungarian artists at the eighth Venice Biennial. It was rejected as ideologically inappropriate due to its portrayal of the communist symbols, but was later used as a poster for Péter Pócs's own exhibition in Paris.

Title: **1989**
Format: **Poster**
Art Director/Designer:
Péter Pócs
Client: **No client**
Country: **Hungary**
Year: **1989**

This self printed poster
for the SZDSZ (Union of
the Free Democrats) was
considered too strong to be
used. The bold graphic
depicts the destruction of
communism and the dates
in the corner refer to the
Hungarian Freedom Flight
(October 23, 1956) and the
eventual collapse of com-
munism in 1989.

Title: **301**
Format: **Poster**
Art Director/Designer:
Péter Pócs
Client: **Union of the Free
Democrats**
Country: **Hungary**
Year: **1989**

Russian troops crushed the
1956 Hungarian Revolution,
killing many Hungarian
citizens and burying them
in mass graves. One of
the graves, in which the
revolutionary leader Imre
Nagy is buried, was marked
with the number 301. The
blood on this poster is in
the shape of Hungary.

Title: **Simile**
Format: **Poster**
Art Director/Designer:
Péter Pócs
Client: **Peter Stefanovits**
Country: **Hungary**
Year: **1988**

This poster, created for an exhibition of graphic designer Peter Stefanovits's work, was shown on Hungarian prime-time news. The news censored the controversial image of the communist star attached to the cross and showed only the text at the bottom.

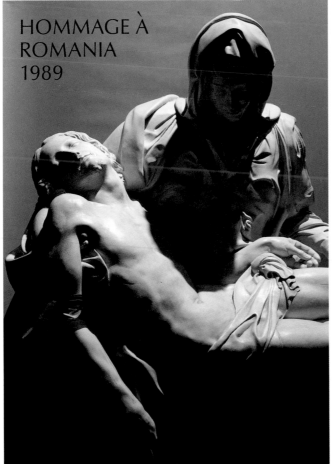

Title: **Hommage à Romania 1989**
Format: **Poster**
Art Director/Designer:
Péter Pócs
Client: **No client**
Country: **Hungary**
Year: **1989**

The famous phrase from the 1960s, "The revolution will be televised," became a reality in 1989. As a result, there was an immediate reaction around the world, and this poster, a response to the Romanian revolution, was already printing on the third day of the bloody event.

Title: **Israeli Law Enforcement**
Format: **Poster**
Art Director/Designer: **Rebecca Rapp**
Client: **"Don't Say You Didn't Know" exhibition curated by Dana Bartelt**
Country: **USA**
Year: **2003**

The designer, an activist for the International Solidarity Movement, illustrates the current situation in Palestine with this powerful image. The design combined the well-known *Pieta* (a symbol for the slain) with a reference to Jesus (who was shown no mercy) to illustrate how history is repeating itself with the slaying of young, innocent Palestinian men. The designer did not intend to make this a religious piece and noted that if another well-known figure had suffered similar treatment, he or she would have been an equally appropriate analogy.

ISRAELI LAW ENFORCEMENT

Since the outbreak of the Intifada in September 2000, approximately 48% of Palestinians killed by Israeli soldiers were males between the ages 19-29; this equates to more than 1320 men. Approximately 61% of all deaths were a result of live ammunition in response to stone-throwing.

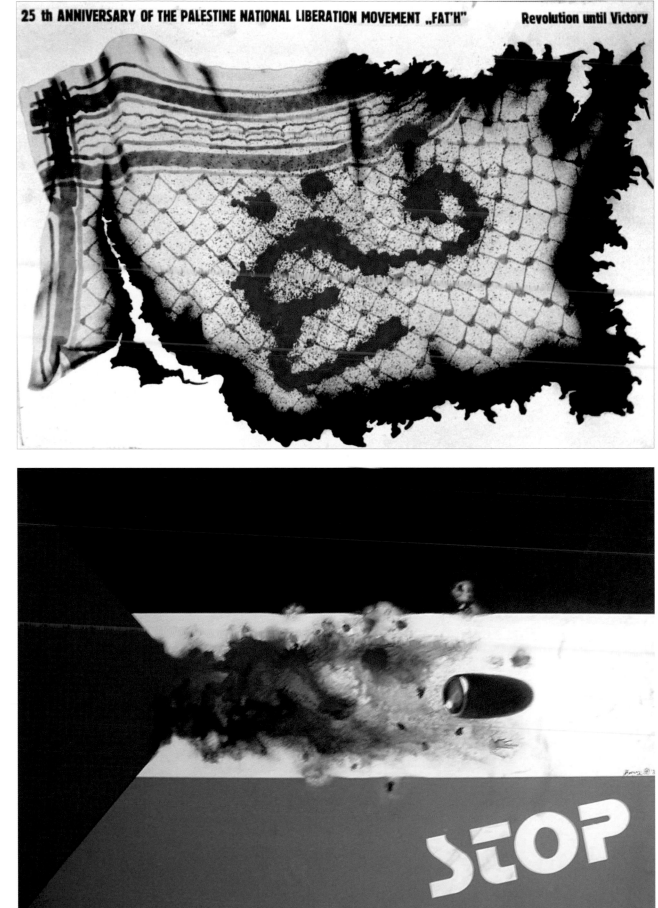

25 th ANNIVERSARY OF THE PALESTINE NATIONAL LIBERATION MOVEMENT „FAT'H"   Revolution until Victory

Title: **Revolution until Victory**
Format: **Poster**
Art Director/Designer: **Unknown**
Client: **No client**
Country: **Poland**
Year: **1989**

The war-torn kaffiyah has the word Fateh in Arabic "blood" red lettering. The kaffiyah was turned into a symbol of the Palestinian state by Yassir Arafat and also became a symbol of the Fedayeen (Palestinian Freedom Fighters).

Title: **Stop**
Format: **Poster**
Art Director/Designer: **Unknown Polish artist, from the collection of Dana Bartelt**
Client: **PLO (Palestine Liberation Organization)**
Country: **Unknown**
Year: **1980s**

In this poster, another one in a series created by Polish artists in solidarity with the Palestinian cause, the Palestine flag is shown pierced by an Israeli sniper's bullet.

STOP

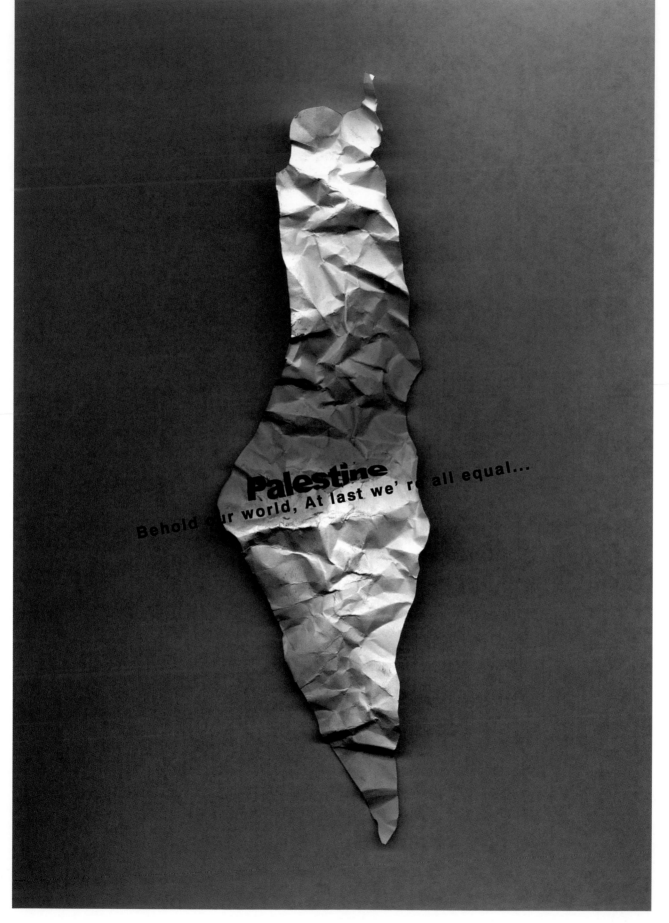

Title: **Palestine**
Format: **Poster**
Art Director/Designer:
Pedram Harby
Client: **No client**
Country: **Iran**
Year: **2004**

The copy line for this poster supporting the Palestinian position states: "Behold our world, At last we're all equal..." The image of a discarded map brought out of the waste basket in an effort "to iron out the creases and restore it to its original place" is persuasive. The designer's idea was to "display the crumpled map of Palestine in the void of indifference that surrounds it." This poster was designed to take part in the 9th triennial of political posters in Mons, Belgium.

Title: **Equal**
Format: **Poster**
Art Director/Designer:
Bülent Erkmen
Client: **Bat Shalom, Israel**
Country: **Turkey**
Year: **1998**

The impossibility of achieving agreement on the mere definition of the word *equal* makes a powerful graphic statement in this poster for the Sharing Jerusalem: Two Capitals project.

Title: **Art Against the Wall**
Format: **Mural**
Art Director/Designers:
Eric Drooker,
Palestinian children
Client: **No client**
Country: **Palestine**
Year: **2004**

The Israeli government calls it "the security barrier." Palestinians call it "the apartheid wall." Twice as tall as the Berlin Wall, its projected span is 500 miles (805 kilometers). The artist calls it "the greatest blank canvas in the world." He painted this mural with the help of local children in the occupied West Bank village of Masha.

Title: **Palestine Is our Home / Stop Israeli Brutality Racism Against Palestinians / End the Occupation of Palestine Now**
Format: **Posters**
Art Director/Designer: **Samia A. Halaby**
Client: **No client**
Country: **USA**
Year: **1991**

The black background and bright colors in *End the Occupation of Palestine Now* and *Palestine Is our Home* are a deliberate homage to Palestinian Libertarian art of the 1970s and 1980s and appeal to the visual requirements of news photographers. These posters were used in Washington, D.C. as protest against the first Gulf War in 1991.

Stop Israeli Brutality Racism Against Palestinians was created to hang in the artist's home to identify her political and ethnic background to visitors. The artist noted that she "did not want to waste time with those who hated my national background . . . ."

Title: **Stone Throwing Boy**
Format: **Poster**
Art Director/Designer:
**Unknown, from the
collection of Dana Bartelt**
Client: **PLO (Palestine
Liberation Organization)**
Country: **Palestine**
Year: **2000**

The Israeli tank is unseen
in this famous photograph
of a Palestinian boy
throwing stones. This
poster was given away by
the Palestinian Liberation
Organization office in
Ramallah during the
second Intifada of 2000.

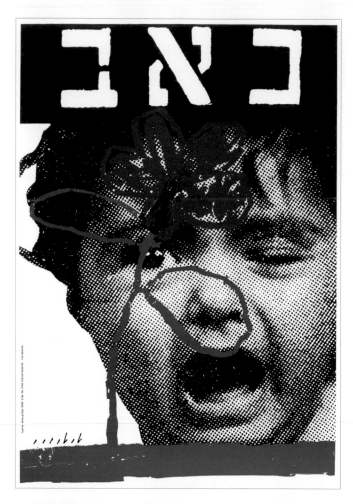

Title: **Pain**
Format: **Poster**
Art Director/Designer:
David Tartakover
Photographer:
Micha Kirshner
Client: **No client**
Country: **Israel**
Year: **1989**

It's almost impossible to imagine how difficult life as an Israeli designer critical of Israeli military behavior must be. Nevertheless, voices consistently opposing the conflict and seeking resolution have emerged. This poster was created for a group of Israelis who refuse to serve their military service in the occupied territories and appeals to others to do the same through this little Palestinian girl who lost an eye to an Israeli rubber bullet. The Hebrew word for "pain" displayed prominently across the top of this poster can also mean "as a father."

Title: **Man Nature Society**
Format: **Poster**
Art Director/Designer:
David Tartakover
Photography: **Alex Levac**
Client: **No client**
Country: **Israel**
Year: **1992**

This poster, designed for the "Man Nature Society" international exhibition held in Moscow, features the colors of the Palestinian flag behind the title blocks.

"It's sad when a child dies, and hard as it is to say it, but he was killed according to regulations" Israel Defence Force spokesman in reaction to the death of 6 year old Ali Muhamad Juarwish, November, 1997.

Title: **Childhood Is Not Child's Play!**
Format: **Poster**
Art Director/Designer: **David Tartakover**
Client: **No client**
Country: **Israel**
Year: **1998**

A quote from an Israeli Defense Forces spokesman explaining that this six-year-old Palestinian boy was "killed according to regulation" offers little comfort, as it remains strikingly apparent that the child pictured here is much too young to stand in the crosshairs of a political battle.

Childhood is not child's play!

THE INTIFADA WELCOMES THE ICOGRADA

Title: **The Intifada Welcomes the Icograda**
Format: **Poster**
Art Director/Designer:
David Tartakover
Client: **No client**
Country: **Israel**
Year: **1989**

Intifada, which literally translates to "an abrupt and sudden waking from an unconscious state," is a word that has come to symbolize the Palestinian uprising against Israeli occupation. More than 11,000 Palestinians have been injured in Intifada protests against Israel. When Icograda, the International Council of Graphic Design Associations, decided to hold its biannual congress in Tel Aviv, this poster was created to announce the conference and remind the international design community that the role of a designer varies with the political climate in which he or she operates.

13th congress of icograda international council of graphic design associations august 27-31 1989 tel aviv

Title: **Happy New Fear**
Format: **Poster**
Art Director/Designer:
David Tartakover
Photographer: **Oded Klein**
Client: **No client**
Country: **Israel**
Year: **1995**

Rather than a stylized version of a weapon, this depiction is starkly realistic. The barrel reads, "Desert Eagle .357 Magnum Pistol—Israel Military Industries," contrasting the harsh reality of Israeli occupation with the festive celebration of a new year. This poster is a reminder that, for many, time only represents a continuation of fear and violence.

Title: **Have a Year of Peace and Security**
Format: **Poster**
Art Director/Designer:
Yossi Lemel
Client: **No client**
Country: **Israel**
Year: **2002**

Irony is an important tool of dissent, but if it lapses into cleverness, the message can be compromised. In this instance, the sense of contrivance may be too evident.

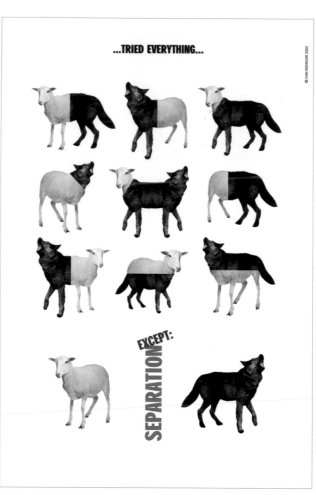

Title: **Separation**
Format: **Poster**
Art Director/Designer:
Dan Reisinger
Client: **No client**
Country: **Israel**
Year: **2003**

After many failed attempts to live in harmony, this poster supports the building of the wall in Israel: "To prevent the infiltration of suicide bombers into Israel and to terminate Israel's intervention into the everyday life of Palestinians."

Title: **F-16i**
Format: **Poster**
Art Director/Designer:
Yossi Lemel
Client: **No client**
Country: **Israel**
Year: **2000**

Critical of the Israeli Air Force, this poster sarcastically suggests that war within the region has become the natural order and the Israeli jet fighter has become another dangerous species.

ISRAEL PALESTINE
ישראל פלשתין 2002

Title: **Blood Bath 2002**
Format: **Poster**
Art Director/Designer:
Yossi Lemel
Client: **No client**
Country: **Israel**
Year: **2002**

This chilling image conveys the designer's opposition to the endless bloodshed between Israelis and Palestinians in which neither side is able to wash away responsibility for the situation. References to morgues and suicides are both intentional and disturbing.

Title: **Israel Palestine 2003**
Format: **Poster**
Art Director/Designer: **Yossi Lemel**
Client: **No client**
Country: **Israel**
Year: **2003**

The imagery in this poster references peace as a living, fragile organism, and questions why Israel's efforts to preserve it, while well intentioned, have not yielded the desired results.

Title: **Israel Palestine 2004**
Format: **Poster**
Art Director/Designer: **Yossi Lemel**
Client: **No client**
Country: **Israel**
Year: **2004**

Depicting a peace process that was brutally cut off in the middle of an attempt to achieve cooperation, this graphic image also references the graphic realities of lost limbs and body parts that are a result of this ongoing conflict.

Title: **Seamline**
Format: **Poster**
Art Director/Designer:
Yossi Lemel
Client: **No client**
Country: **Israel**
Year: **2001**

Context creates meaning. This image of raw meat bound together by string could almost appear in a cookbook as an example of how to tie a roast. When placed into the context of the seamline—the border between the Israeli and Palestinian territories—the meaning darkens. The subtle color variation between the two sides intentionally and cleverly reflects the skin tones of those involved.

Title: *Dani* magazine
Format: **Magazine covers**
Art Director/Designer:
Trio Sarajevo
Client: *DANI* **magazine**
Country: **Bosnia
and Herzegovina**
Year: **1995**

DANI magazine, the
political weekly considered
to be the most courageous
magazine in Sarajevo
during the siege,
consistently produced
provocative covers. On this
cover Radovan Karadzic,
the former President of the
Republica Srpska accused
of the slaughter of thou-
sands of Bosnian Muslims
and Croats who has twice
been indicted by the United
Nations war crimes tribu-
nal, is shown opposite Adolf
Hitler indicating their similar style of "leadership."

These front and back
covers of *DANI* magazine
question whether the new
unification into two
separate states, the Bosnian
Republic and the Serbian
Republic, according to
Dayton accord, have
achieved the designed
objectives.

This horrifying image depicting the results of a Serbian mortar explosion that landed near a market square is almost too much to bear. This event, and the published images from it, caused foreign governments to finally take action.

These images of Muslim families being expelled from Serbian controlled territories in Bosnia are evidence of the ethnic cleansing that took place in the mid 1990s.

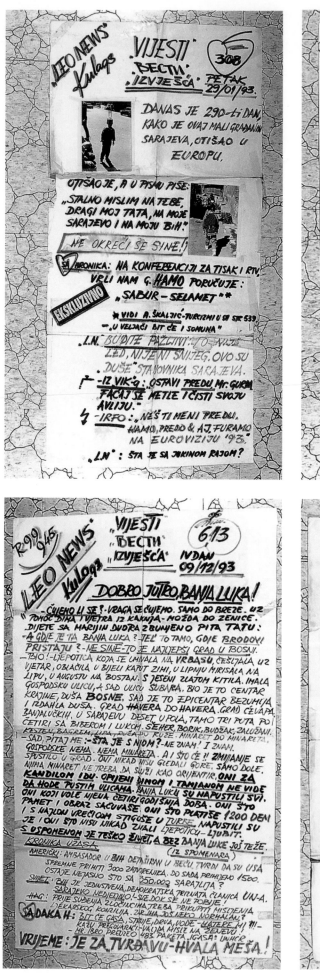

Title: *Leo News*
Format: Handwritten
posters
Art Director/Designer:
Malik "Kula" Kulenović
Client: No client
Country: Bosnia
and Herzegovina
Year: 1993–94

Numbering each edition
of this handwritten
newspaper with the day of
the siege of Sarajevo
increased the political
power of this publication
produced by a news vendor.
Each edition combined
Cyrillic and Roman
alphabets, making a
poignant plea for ethnic
unity. The use of the two
alphabets turned out to
be as significant as the
news itself.

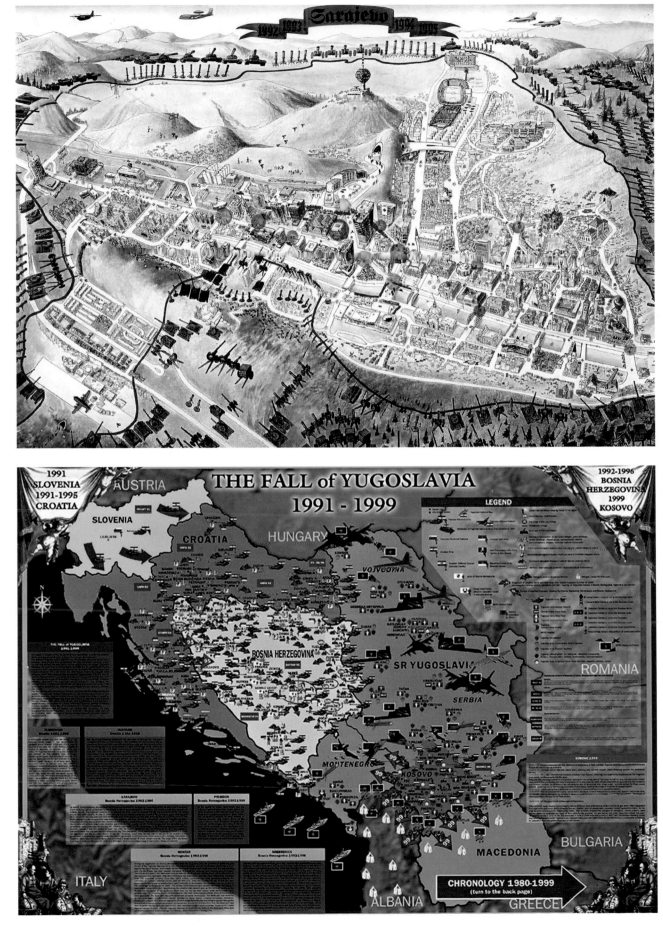

Title: Survival Map '92–'96
Format: Poster
Art Directors/Designers:
Suada Kapić,
Emir Kasumagić
Illustrator: Ozren Pavlović
Photographer:
Drago Resner
Client:
FAMA International
Country: Bosnia and Herzegovina
Year: 1996

The romance and beauty of an old hand-drawn map of Sarajevo is appropriated by the illustrator showing us instead the tragedy of the long siege, which lasted 1,395 days—the longest in modern times. This commemorative map details the horror of being a city set snuggly in the mountains with a vast array of artillery, ready to demolish it at a moment's notice. This poster has been sold and distributed around the world and is said to be displayed at the International Criminal Tribunal office in the Hague.

Title: The Fall of Yugoslavia 1991–1999, causes and consequences
Format: Map
Art Directors/Designers:
Miran Norderland,
Jelena Vranić
Client:
FAMA International
Country: Bosnia and Herzegovina
Year: 1999

This ambitious work documents the events that occurred in the former Yugoslavia between 1991 and 1999. When the Kosovo crisis and conflict started, the designer realized the need for connecting all the events in order to explain that Kosovo was not an isolated conflict, but a consequence of the 1991–1995 wars that concluded with the Dayton Peace Accords. It has been distributed around the world as a teaching aid and a "contribution for national truth and reconciliation and democratization of the post war society."

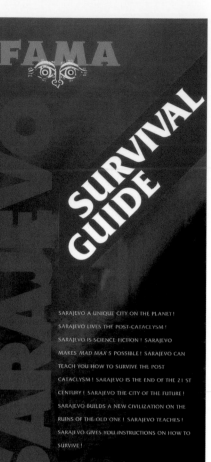

FAMA

SARAJEVO

SURVIVAL GUIDE

SARAJEVO A UNIQUE CITY ON THE PLANET !
SARAJEVO LIVES THE POST-CATACLYSM !
SARAJEVO IS SCIENCE FICTION ! SARAJEVO
MAKES *MAD MAX 5* POSSIBLE ! SARAJEVO CAN
TEACH YOU HOW TO SURVIVE THE POST
CATACLYSM ! SARAJEVO IS THE END OF THE 21 ST
CENTURY ! SARAJEVO THE CITY OF THE FUTURE !
SARAJEVO BUILDS A NEW CIVILIZATION ON THE
RUINS OF THE OLD ONE ! SARAJEVO TEACHES !
SARAJEVO GIVES YOU INSTRUCTIONS ON HOW TO
SURVIVE !

Title: *Survival Guide*
Format: **Book**
Author: **Suada Kapić**
Designer: **Boris Dogan**
Client:
FAMA International
Country: **Bosnia
and Herzegovina**
Year: **1993**

Or, everything tastes better than the boiled water. And, what are we going to do once all trees are gone?

Birch-juice
Young birch tree should be drilled. In the hole a few centimeters deep, one should install a tube. Leave it for forty-eight hours, while the juice is being collected in a tin. During April and May, one can get 8 liters of juice during 48 hours. Juice can be mixed with wine, sugar, yeast or lemon, and then left to ferment. This process demands several days.

Fir-tree-juice
Cut the needles of young fir-tree, and keep them in hot water for two or three minutes. Then cut them in tiny pieces, press, and put in cold water for two or three hours. If days are sunny, keep the jar in the sun. Filter and sweeten before serving. Pine-tree and juniper-tree can do just as well.

Boza
Once well known and very popular refreshment, gone out of style. Could be found only in two or three pastry-shops on Baščaršija.
0.5 kilos of corn flour
1 package of yeast
8 l of water
sugar and lemon-powder, if you have it and as you like it.
Put the corn flour in some water and leave it for 24 hours. Then cook it on a low heat about two hours, mixing occasionally and adding water. When it cools of, add the yeast and leave for 24 hours. Then add sugar and lemon-powder, leave it for three more hours and add 8 to 10 liters of water. Should be served cold.

Non-alcoholic beverages

Alcoholic beverages

Sarajevo cognac
3-4 spoons of sugar
water
ethyl alcohol
The quality of cognac depends on the brand of alcohol and on the quality of the Sarajevo water, preferably brought from some of the protected wells. Fry the sugar, add some water to melt it, and bring to a boil. Mix the water and alcohol in a ratio of 2.5:1, and add the sugar.

Wine
1/2 kilo of sugar
5 l of boiled water
1/2 kilo of rice
1 pack of yeast
10 cl of alcohol, or 20 cl of rum
Mix all the ingredients, and pour them in hermetically closed canister. Ten days later, extract the wine through a Melita coffee-filter.

Saki
5 l of water
0.5 kilos of rice
0.5 kilos of sugaryeast
Should sit for seven days and ferment. Then filter the drink and use rice in the pie.

This book was created to document the survival tactics used during the siege of Sarajevo to facilitate everyday needs, such as heating buildings, making alcohol, and taking care of sick animals. The writers wanted to pass their hard-earned knowledge onto others who may one day experience similar events. Kapić was taken out of Bosnia during the siege by the Japanese government in order to promote this book. After, she returned to Bosnia, still under siege.

Medical care

Medical care: its main characteristic is very friendly personnel, which was not the case before the war. It is very efficient. Aside from the hospital and emergency rooms, you will hear quickly about all the improvised ambulances. The maternity hospital has been shelled and is out of use, so babies are born in the regular hospital. When visiting the dentist, you should take your bottle with water, and gloves, which she can use while treating you.

Pharmacies are working, but medicine is mostly missing. Bring your own vitamins. In emergency — look for the locations of Benevolencija and Caritas.

Veterinarian's Clinic

The Veterinarian's Clinic is on Daniel Ozmo Street, in the store where they used to sell hi-fi equipment. Its hours are from 9 a.m. and 2 p.m. Lines are very long, and the service is full, including very complex surgical operations. Sarajevo became the city of abandoned pedigree dogs who are sadly roaming the streets, frozen, hungry and wounded. Their owners have left Sarajevo and left them behind, or they don't have food to even feed themselves.

Cemeteries

The beauty of old Sarajevo cemeteries has been ruined by growing needs. They have been reopened when two contemporary cemeteries — Bare and Vlakovo — became inaccessible. Small old cemeteries which were active for certain neighborhoods, even streets (mahalska) were closed in 1878, with the arrival of the Austro-Hungarian Empire. More than a century later, they started functioning again. People are being buried next to the mosques, on playgrounds in front of their houses. The old military cemeteries — Austrian, of the First Yugoslavia, German, and a partisan one — are full. Since September, the small stadium in the sports complex Koševo, was turned into a cemetery, too. Funerals are held in early morning or dusk hours, to avoid the shelling. There is a rule not to go to the funerals and not to have flowers and wreaths. They cannot be bought anyway, even if someone would want to.

No teeth...?
A mustache...?
smel like shit...?

Bosnian girl

Šejla Kamerić
Graffiti written by an unknown Dutch soldier on an army barracks wall in Potočari, Srebrenica, 1994/95.
Royal Netherlands Army troops, as part of the UN Protection Force (UNPROFOR) in Bosnia
and Herzegovina 1992–95, were responsible for protecting the Srebrenica safe area.
Photograpy by Tarik Samarah

Title: **Bosnian Girl**
Format: **Poster**
Art Director/Designer:
Šejla Kamerić
Photographer:
Tarik Samarah
Client: **No client**
Country: **Bosnia and Herzegovina**
Year: **Graffiti: 1994/1995, Poster: 2003**

Contemptuous graffiti written by an unknown soldier from the Royal Netherlands Army troops was found and photographed in a factory used by the troops as a U.N. Protection Forces barracks during the siege of Srebrenica (a building later used by Serbs to execute Bosnians.) This graffiti clearly explains the attitudes and failure of the U.N. forces responsible for protecting the safe area. The artist positioned this found graffiti over an image of a Bosnian girl to illustrate the Srebrenica tragedy and the prejudice Bosnians faced, as well as the prejudice Bosnians have toward others. The work was a public project and was used on posters, billboards, magazine ads, and postcards.

Title: *Mladina*
Format: **Magazine cover**
Art Director/Designer:
Trio Sarajevo
Client: *Mladina* magazine
Country: **Slovenia**
Year: **1995**

A collaged image showing
UN Secretary-General
Boutros Boutros Galli
kissing the lower back side
of the Yugoslav-Serbian
President Slobodon
Milosevic was featured on
the cover of *Mladina*
magazine because the
United Nations did not
want to take a strong stand
on the Yugoslavian-Serbian
atrocities in Bosnia.

Title: **UNable**
Format: **Poster**
Art Director/Designer:
Yossi Lemel
Client: **No client**
Country: **Israel**
Year: **1995**

In this political poster, the
artist chose a helpless,
impotent turtle on its back
to symbolize the United
Nations (UN), after its inef-
fective attempt to resolve
conflict in Bosnia.

Made in Bosnia

Title: **Made in Bosnia**
Format: **Poster**
Art Director/Designer:
Anur Hadziomerspahić
Client: **No client**
Country: **Bosnia
and Hertzegovina**
Year: **1998**

The numerous European
campaigns protesting the
killing of animals incited
this campaign against the
killing of humans in Bosnia.

Title: **Bosnian Postcards**
Format: **Postcard**
Art Director/Designer:
Anur Hadziomerspahić
Client: **No client**
Country: **Bosnia
and Hertzegovina**
Year: **1998**

This postcard (*right*)
reflects the three etnic
and religious groups
(Serbs, Croats, Muslims)
that are fighting together
as one army. By showing
their private parts, they
are showing their ethnic
diversity. Because Muslims
are the only group that
circumcise their men, in the
past conflicts this has been
a way of identifying them.

After the war, a portion of
the population turned
toward faith in a more
aggressive and expressive
manner than they had in
the recent past.

Title: **Sarajevo Humor**
Format: **Poster**
Art Director/Designer:
Anur Hadziomerspahić
Client: **No client**
Country: **Bosnia
and Hertzegovina**
Year: **1998**

Tens of thousands of limbs
have been destroyed by
landmines. As a result,
Bosnia is currently the
world champion in sitting
volleyball.

Title: **Sarajevo Postcard
Collection**
Format: **Postcards**
Art Director/Designers:
Trio Sarajevo
Client: **No client**
Country: **Bosnia
and Herzegovina**
Year: **1993**

To convey the idea of
suffering in Sarajevo, artists
used any available images
including pop and visual
icons.

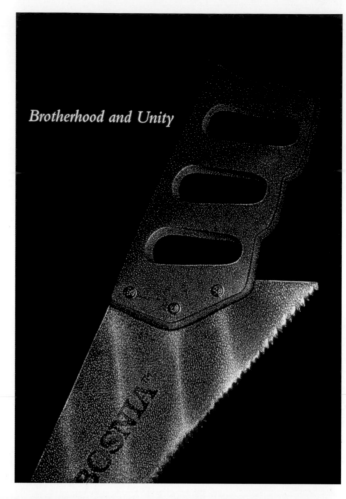

Title: **Brotherhood
and Unity**
Format: **Poster**
Art Director/Designer:
Cedomir Kostović
Client: **Southwest
Missouri State University**
Country: **USA**
Year: **1994**

The three-holed handle of
this bloody saw signifies
the three ethnic and
religious groups (Serbs,
Croats, and Muslims)
contributing to the
destruction and devastation
of Bosnia. "Brotherhood
and Unity" was a
communist slogan used to
keep the groups united.
This poster suggests that
what they are actually
working together to
accomplish is the
destruction of Bosnia.

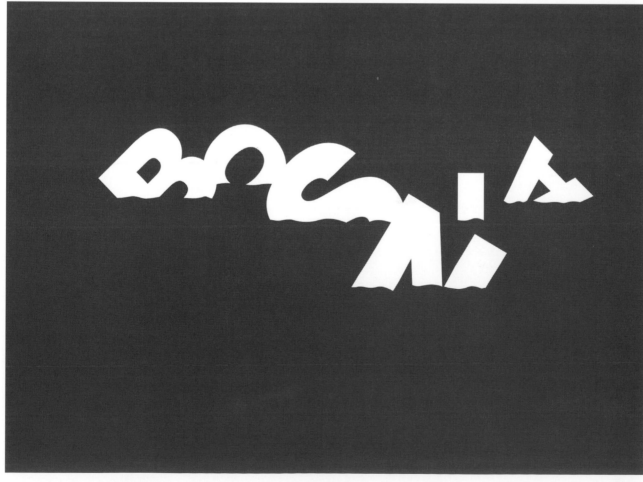

Title: **Bosnia
(Sea of Blood)**
Format: **Poster**
Art Director/Designer:
Cedomir Kostović
Client: **Southwest
Missouri State University**
Country: **USA**
Year: **1994**

This strong and effective
use of typography suggests
that at the time this poster
was designed, Bosnia was
drowning in a sea of blood.

Title: **Bosnia (Divided)**
Format: **Poster**
Art Director/Designer:
Cedomir Kostović
Client: **Southwest
Missouri State University**
Country: **USA**
Year: **1994**

The division of Bosnia is
represented by this violin,
now in three pieces, which
has been dismantled and
made into a useless object,
no longer capable of
creating music. For
Bosnia/the violin to work
again, the country's three
religious groups (Serbs,
Croats, and Muslims) must
reunite and work together.

Title: **Glazbeni Dozivljaji**
Format: **Poster**
Art Director/Designer/
Illustrator: **Boris Bućan**
Client: **Zagrebački
Simfoničari I Zbor HRTV**
Country: **Croatia**
Year: **1990–91**

This series of posters was
created for the Zagreb
Philharmonic Orchestra
just prior to, and during
the beginning of, the
Serbo/Croatian war. The
illustrations subtly depict a
war within an orchestra by
showing musicians fighting
against each other.

Title: Wa
Format:
Art Dire
Mirko II
Client: 1
Country
Year: 19

This fol
hold inf
Los Ang
event to
the war

Title: S
Format
Art Dire
Ranko
Client:
Club Lj
Countr
Year: 19

This po
checker
of Croa
times, s
splatter
SOS (M
signal)
aggress
(bottom

Title: K
Forma
and T-
Art Di
Boris
Client:
Count
Year: 1

This p
pay at
clever
in "Hr
spellir
get its
chang
Croat
"krv"
(botto

Title: **Read Between the Lines**
Format: **Poster**
Art Director/Designer: **Boris Ljubicić**
Client: **No client**
Country: **Croatia**
Year: **1994**

The text on this poster, designed to be read from a short distance, was written by the survivors of the massacre of Vukovar, sometimes known as the Croatian Stalingrad because of its total destruction. The piece commemorating the third anniversary of the occupation of Vukovar, in which 700 of its defenders and 1,600 civilians were killed, and 2,600 of its inhabitants disappeared without a trace, asks for the liberation and return of its people.

Title: **Serbian Cutting**
Format: **Magazine**
Art Director/Designers: **Dejan Krsić, Dejan Dragosavac Rutta**
Client: *Bastard* **magazine**
Country: **Slovenia and Serbia**
Year: **1998**

New Moment (visual communications, design, and arts magazine) offered the designers space to promote their magazine for free, so the designers wanted to use that opportunity to raise awareness about crimes of official Serbian politics on Kosovo. They cleverly chose a headline that refers to avant-garde film montage in Serbian cinema as well as images of the atrocities being committed against Albanian citizens in Kosovo. Subsequently, the design was rejected by *New Moment*, but was later published in the first issue of *Bastard* magazine.

Title: Mi smo se borili
da bi se vi danas borili
Format: Poster
Art Director/Designers:
Albino Ursić, Boris Kuk
Client: No client
Country: Croatia
Year: 1993

This photograph of World
War II partisan fighters,
combined with the
message "we fought (for
unity) so you can fight (to
break apart) now," is a
sarcastic jab at the struggle
between various groups in
Croatia. The text at the top
of the poster reads "Party
of recovered partisans."

Mi smo se borili da bi se vi danas borili

Title: Fascist Groove
Format: Poster
and postcard
Art Director/Designer:
Dejan Krsić
Client: Self, NGO
"Moj Glas"
Country: Croatia
Year: 2002

Posters and postcards take
the theme from the song of
a German rock band named
Heaven 17: "We don't need
this fascist groove thing."
The cover text accuses the
political party HDZ of
promoting intolerance.
The postcard, featuring the
Prime Minister holding his
right hand in the air, comes
preprinted with the address
of the Croatian parliament
on the back (right) so the
reader can easily send it.
This work was done during
the Croatian general's trial
at the Hague International
Court for War Crimes.

www.mojglas.org

Ja dižem svoj glas
PROTIV: nacionalne
NETRPELJIVOSTI, rasne
netrpeljivosti, šovinizma,
seksizma, kao i svih oblika
MRŽNJE koji se promoviraju
na prosvjednim skupovima u
organizaciji Stožera za obranu
digniteta Mirka NORCA.

OSUĐUJEM: negiranje
pravne države, kao i poticanje
na legalizaciju zločina u
ime hrvatskog naroda!

moj saborski zastupnik/ica

Sabor RH
Trg Sv Marka 6
HR-10000 Zagreb

MOJ POTPIS

kosovo
risiko

Gioko di guerra

Title: **Kosovo Risiko**
Format: **Poster**
Art Director/Designer:
Andrea Rauch
Client: **No client**
Country: **Italy**
Year: **1999**

Created in opposition to
the war in Kosovo, this
poster uses a play on words
between Kosovo and Risiko,
a popular Italian "gioko di
guerra," or war game.

L´impossible

Title: **L'impossible**
Format: **Flyer**
Art Director/Designer:
Stanislav Sharp
Client: **Art Group FIA**
Country: **Serbia
and Montenegro**
Year: **1993**

This flyer, which was
distributed in Serbia,
featured an image of
Serbian soldiers riding
through the ruined, a.k.a.
"liberated," streets of
Vukovar, proving that
soldiers from Serbia took
part in the war in Croatia,
a fact that was not
acknowledged by the
Serbian media.

Dragoljub Zamurović, Oslobađanje Vukovara, 1991. (GAMMA PRESS IMAGE; PARIS MATCH)

ΦΟΤΟΓΡΑΦΙΑ
FOTOGRAFIE

БЕОГРАД BELGRADE

9

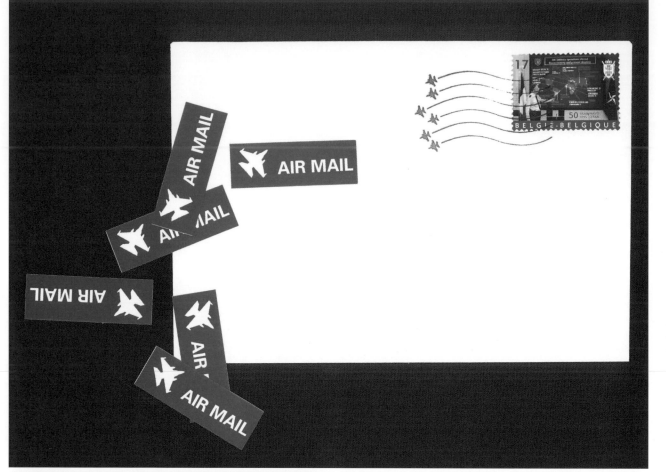

Title: **Airmail**
Format: **Airmail sticker**
Art Director/Designers:
Lisa Boxus and Skart
Client: **No client**
Country: **Belgium**
Year: **1999**

The simple substitution of
a fighter plane effectively
transforms the airmail
sticker into a warning that
no one can stay out of
politics. FRONT is an art
activism against violence
group, which is based in
Brussels and was initiated
by Skart who distributed
these as an act of civil dis-
obedience.

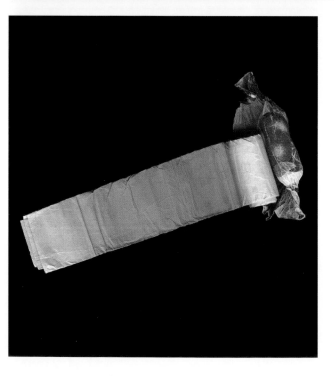

BANG!

(YOU ARE DEAD)

Title: **Bombon**
Format: **Candy wrapper**
Art Director/Designers:
**Philippe Hulet
and Skart**
Client: **No client**
Country: **Belgium**
Year: **1999**

The desirability of imported
Belgium bonbons is lost
upon the opening of a
"Bombon," which appears
to be a wrapped candy, but
is actually a rolled piece
of paper revealing the sad
reality of NATO participating in war instead of
providing humanitarian
aid. The Bombons
were distributed during
the NATO aggression of
Yugoslavia in 1999.

Title: **Postcards
to Milošević**
Format: **Postcards**
Art Director/Designer:
Nikola Kostandinović
Client:
Organization Otpor
Country: **Serbia
and Montenegro**
Year: **2000**

Organization Otpor is
an independent,
nongovernmental
organization whose
activists played a crucial
role in the street
demonstrations that began
immediately following
the elections and led to
Slobodan Milošević's
downfall. "Otpor" in
Serbian means "resistance,"
and the organization was
founded in the mid-1990s
by students from Belgrade
University and elsewhere
in Serbia, who had had
enough of Milošević's
chokehold on the neck
of the Serbian society.
Between 1999 and 2001,
more than 1,500 Otpor
activists (of about 50,000
based in more than ten
Serbian cities) were arrested
and interrogated by security
forces under Milošević's
control. This series of postcards mocking Milošović
was pre-addressed to be
sent to Milošević's home.

Gospodine Miloševiću,
Posle deset godina
nesreće koju ste Vi doneli
bivšoj Jugoslaviji,
Srbiji i srpskom narodu,
vreme je da se povučete
dok ne bude kasno za
Vas i za nas.

UPUTSTVO:
Ukoliko se slažete sa ovom porukom
samo zalepite poštansku marku,
potpišite se i ovu razglednicu ubacite
u prvo poštansko sanduče.

G-din Slobodan
Milošević
11000 Beograd
Užička 16
Srbija

Got oil?

Title: **Got Oil?**
Format: **Poster**
Art Director/Designers:
Nenad Cizl, Toni Tomašek
Client: **Magdalena Young
Creatives Festival**
Country: **Slovenia**
Year: **2004**

Part of the power of this
poster depends on the
viewer's knowledge of the
"Got Milk?" ad campaign
for the American Dairy
Association in which the
subjects featured are
always shown with a "milk
mustache." In this parody,
Bush's lips are smeared
with oil creating a
vampirelike image, alluding
to his passion for oil.

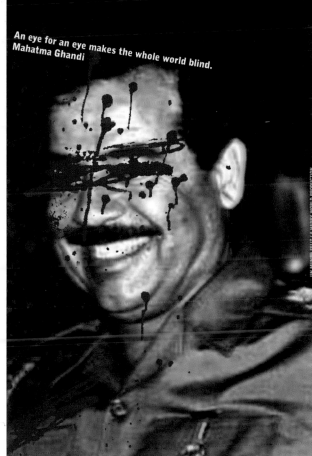

Title: **Blind**
Format: **Digital postcards**
Art Director/Designers
Sonia Freeman,
Gabriel Freeman
Client: **Un Mundo Feliz/A**
Happy World Production
Country: **Spain**
Year: **2003**

These posters were created
for an exhibition in
Portland, Oregon entitled:
"The Language of Terror:
anti-war.us graphics" in
which all works were
wildposted to a single wall.
The first two images create
a parallel between Bush's
and Saddam's blindness in
the war, and the final image
reflects how we were all
affected by their blindness.

BIG OIL, EXPLOITING U.S. FOREIGN POLICY SINCE 2001.
Prior to becoming president, George W. Bush honed his executive skills by driving three oil exploration corporations to financial ruin. Now, he's determined to do the same to America.

BIG OIL, LUBRICATING U.S. FOREIGN POLICY SINCE 2001.
Former Halliburton CEO and current U.S. vice president, Dick Cheney, still receives deferred salary from Halliburton—the world's largest oil field services corporation.

BIG OIL, FUELING U.S. FOREIGN POLICY SINCE 2001.
Former director of Chevron, Condoleezza Rice accepted the highest honor Chevron could bestow—a supertanker named Condoleezza Rice.

BIG OIL, THE SANCTIONED WMD OF U.S. FOREIGN POLICY.
The Bush administration blatantly disregarded U.N. policy, ignored world protest and bullied Iraq. The true smoking gun is not Iraqi WMD, but big oil.

Title: **Big Oil**
Format: **Poster series**
Art Director/Designer:
May L. Sorum
Client: **No client**
Country: **USA**
Year: **2004**

The Big Oil poster series uses oil-splattered portraits of George Bush, Dick Cheney, and Condoleezza Rice to draw parallels between the oil interests of the Bush Administration and American political policy. At the bottom of each poster, direct connections between the people featured and the oil industry are simply stated.

America, where have you gone?

Title: **Death Flag (America, Where Have You Gone?)**
Format: **Poster**
Art Director/Designer: **Adrienne Burk**
Client: **No client**
Country: **USA**
Year: **2003**

In this bold and simple image, the designer creates an American flag out of blood and oil, suggesting America has forgotten constitutional ideals. The poster was used at anti-Iraq war protests.

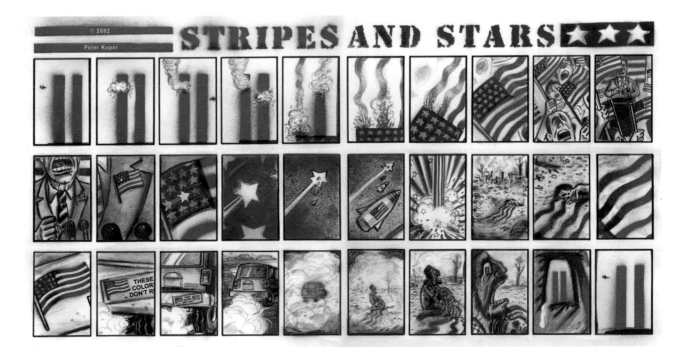

Title: **Stripes and Stars**
Format: **Comic**
Art Director/Designer: **Carrie Whitney**
Illustrator: **Peter Kuper**
Client:
The Comics Journal
Country: **USA**
Year: **2002**

This comic strip was created for the special patriotism issue of *The Comics Journal*, a vigorous antagonist of the Bush Administration, suggesting how an endless war on terrorism would create an endless cycle of violence.

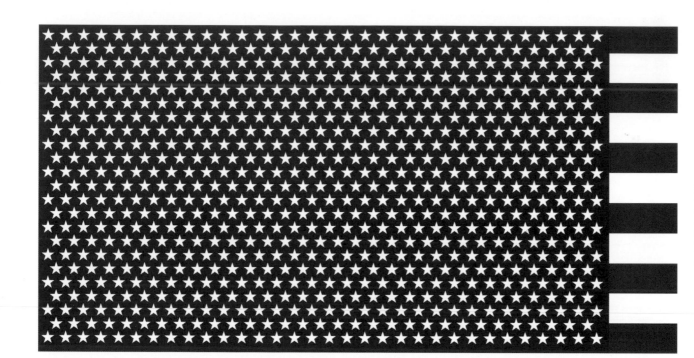

Title: **American Flag**
Format: **Poster**
Art Director/Designers:
Nenad Cizl, Toni Tomašek
Client: *Mladina* **magazine**
Country: **Slovenia**
Year: **2003**

In this poster commenting on American politics around the globe, the American flag shown has grown from 50 stars, each representing a state within the United States, to an innumerable number.

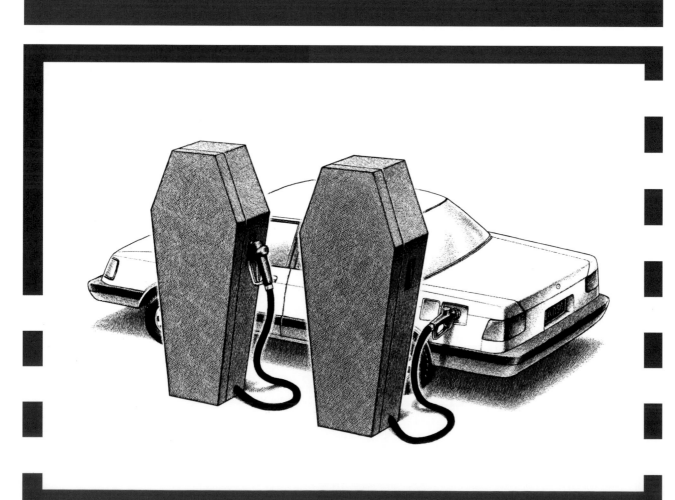

Title: **Fuel**
Format: **Poster**
Art Director/Designer:
Mirko Ilić
Client: **No client**
Country: **USA**
Year: **1990**

Originally created as a *New York Times* op-ed illustration on the 1990 Gulf War, additional elements including the American flag made this a suitable image for anti-war protests in Washington, D.C. in 2003.

Title: **Guided Missiles**
Format: **Postcard**
Art Director/Designer:
Joe Miller
Client:
AnotherPosterForPeace.org
Country: **USA**
Year: **2003**

The powerful quote by Martin Luther King, Jr. comparing "guided missiles" to "misguided men" is paralleled by a strong image of missiles imposed on the Earth. This bold imagery indicates that our technology of destruction has redefined the way conflicts are resolved and that "humanity and weaponry are set at odds."

Title: **USA in Irak. Not to War**
Format: **Poster**
Art Director/Designer:
Renato Aranda Rodríguez
Client: **No client**
Country: **Mexico**
Year: **2003**

By transforming a map of the United States into a meat cleaver, the designer makes a powerful comment on the U.S. bombing of Iraq. The first information received in Mexico at the beginning of the war was that the attacks were "surgical," a reference to the precision of the missiles. This work speaks to the arrogance of the term, as "there is no war where only the bad people die."

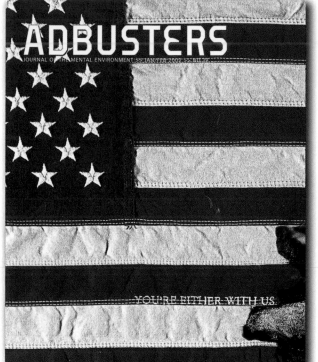

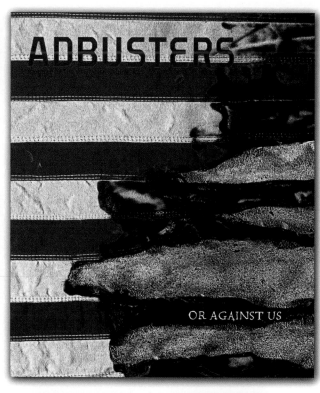

Title: *Adbusters*
Issue #39
Format: **Magazine cover**
Art Director/Designer:
**Adbusters
Media Foundation**
Photographer:
Randall Cosco
Client: *Adbusters*
Country: **Canada**
Year: **2002**

This issue was the first published after September 11, 2001. The gravity of the event caused the magazine to shift its focus slightly, with subsequent issues placing more emphasis on U.S. foreign policy. *(top)*

Title: Will Kill for Oil
Format: **T-shirt**
Client: **No client**
Art Director/Designer:
Christopher Loch
Country: **USA**
Year: **2004**

A satirical design based on the phrase "Will work for food" has been used for T-shirts, postcards, and stickers. The posture of a begging Bush reminds everyone that the continuing cooperation of Americans is needed to sustain his policies.
(bottom left)

Title: Oil Habit
Format: **T-shirt**
Art Director/Designers:
**Scott Palmer,
Keeno Ahmed**
Client: **No client**
Country: **USA**
Year: **2004**

This skull comprising 1,000 oil rigs, comments on the global dependency for oil and its disastrous effects politically and environmentally.
(bottom right)

Title: **First Killing/Oil Spill**
Format: **Leaflets**
Art Director/Designer:
Dennis Edge
Client: **No client**
Country: **USA**
Year: **2004**

These two images were part of a series of leaflets alerting people about the dangerous consequences of irresponsible oil consumption. *(top)*

Title: **War on Terror**
Format: **Poster**
Art Director/Designers:
**Marty Neumeier,
Josh Levine**
Client:
AnotherPosterForPeace.org
Country: **USA**
Year: **2004**

In response to the events of September 11, this poster aptly suggests "applying technological violence to terrorism is like pouring gas on a fire...the viewer knows exactly what to expect if the gas is poured." *(top right)*

Title: **anti-war.us**
Format: **Website**
Art Director/Curator:
Joshua Berger
Designer: **Jon Steinhorst**
Interface designer:
Anthony Ramos
Client: **No client**
Country: **USA**
Year: **2002**

The anti-war.us website was created by Plazm Design to distribute effective anti-war messages and graphics to activists around the world. The intention is to make the images available to the public for downloading so that they can be transferred to stickers, posters, signs, or other media for posting. *(bottom)*

Title: **War on Iraq?**
Format: **Billboard**
Art Director/Designer:
Noah Scalin
Client: **Richmond Peace Coalition**
Country: USA
Year: 2003

"Not in our name" became a phrase used by the peace movement before the war in Iraq was initiated. The campaign was originally planned as a series of billboards with a variety of messages but reverted to a single location after the original billboard company refused to run the series due to its content. *(top)*

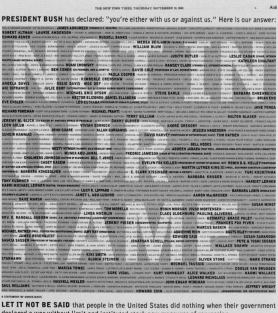

Title: **Not In Our Name**
Format: **Newspaper ad**
Art Director/Designers:
Sheila Levrant de Bretteville, Scott Stowell, Susan Barber
Client: **Not In Our Name**
Country: USA
Year: 2002

Not In Our Name is a coalition of Americans dedicated to peace and civil liberties for all. This full-page newspaper ad features the Not In Our Name Statement of Conscience and the names of some of the thousands of people who support this open letter to George Bush/ad which was published in the *New York Times* on September 19, 2002. *(bottom left)*

Title: **Don't Buy It.**
Format: **Poster**
Art Director/Designer:
Kimberly Cross
Client:
AnotherPosterForPeace.org
Country: USA
Year: 2003

By asking viewers to boycott the war, the artist is commenting on the notion that the war was sold to the American public as if it were a product. *(bottom right)*

Title: *The Nation*
Initiative Buttons
Format: **Buttons**
Art Director/Designer:
Milton Glaser
Client: *The Nation*
magazine
Country: **USA**
Year: **2003-2004**

This series of pre-Iraq war buttons were sold by the *The Nation* to its readers and were widely circulated.

Title: *2/15: The Day the World Said No to War*
Format: **Book**
Art Director/Designer:
Connie Koch
Client: **Hello [NYC],
All Press**
Country: **USA**
Year: **2003**

Thirty million people in thirty-eight countries gathered to protest the imminent U.S. invasion of Iraq on February 15, 2003. The photographs and comments were collected via email and used to produce the book *2/15*. The designers hope this reminder of the pressure that civil power can exert on governments will inspire continued involvement.

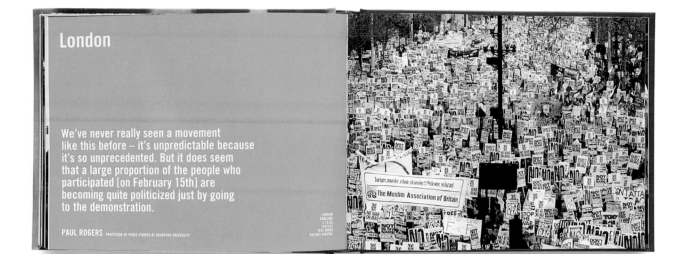

London

We've never really seen a movement like this before – it's unpredictable because it's so unprecedented. But it does seem that a large proportion of the people who participated [on February 15th] are becoming quite politicized just by going to the demonstration.

PAUL ROGERS PROFESSOR OF PEACE STUDIES AT BRADFORD UNIVERSITY

LONDON
ENGLAND
2.15.03
PHOTO BY
JESS HURD
REPORT DIGITAL

BYRON BAY
AUSTRALIA
2.2.03
PHOTO BY
PETER & LISA GARRETTE
ICON IMAGES PTY LTD
NUDE NO WAR PROTEST

WASHINGTON D.C.
USA
2.15.03
PHOTO BY
SONDA DAWES
THE IMAGE WORKS

Our Nation's cause has always been larger than our Nation's defense. We fight, as we always fight, for a just peace – a peace that favors liberty. We will defend the peace against the threats from terrorists and tyrants. We will preserve the peace by building good relations among the great powers. And we will extend the peace by encouraging free and open societies on every continent.

GEORGE W. BUSH
PRESIDENT OF THE UNITED STATES OF AMERICA ON THE NATIONAL SECURITY STRATEGY OF THE UNITED STATES, 6.1.2002

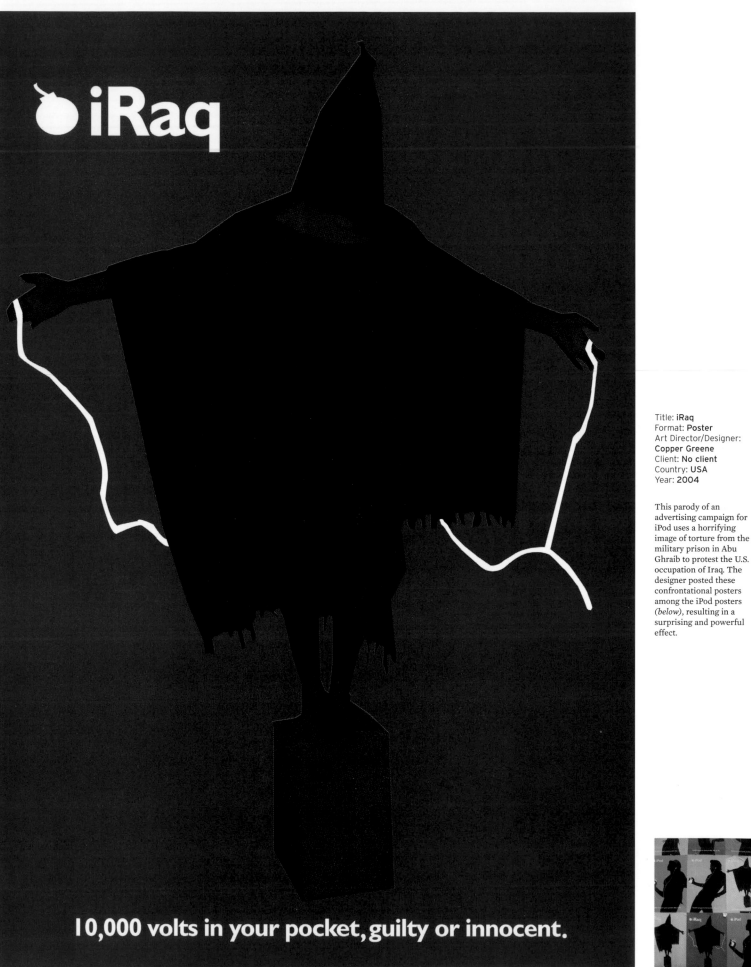

Title: **iRaq**
Format: **Poster**
Art Director/Designer:
Copper Greene
Client: **No client**
Country: **USA**
Year: **2004**

This parody of an
advertising campaign for
iPod uses a horrifying
image of torture from the
military prison in Abu
Ghraib to protest the U.S.
occupation of Iraq. The
designer posted these
confrontational posters
among the iPod posters
(below), resulting in a
surprising and powerful
effect.

Title: **Non-Suicide Bomber**
Format: **Postcard**
Art Director/Designer:
Chaz Maviyane-Davies
Client: **No client**
Country: **USA**
Year: **2004**

This piece was inspired by a radio interview the designer heard in which an Iraqi ironically referred to the actions of the United States as "non-suicide bombers."

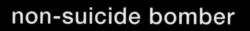

non-suicide bomber

Title: **Victory?**
Format: **Poster**
Art Director/Designer:
Jadran Boban
Client: **Syracuse
Anti-War Demo**
Country: **Croatia**
Year: **2003**

An ironic victory is shown
by using the most popular
symbol of the Second
World War to create the
message that every war
victory leaves death behind.
The work, created for
anti-war demonstrations in
Syracuse, New York, was
distributed over the
Internet and taped up
around the city as a call to
and promotion for
demonstrations.

Title: **Alternative Street Sign**
Format: **Poster series**
Art Director/Designer: **Michael Duffy**
Client: **No client**
Country: **USA**
Year: **2003**

This series of stenciled signs was surreptitiously affixed to traffic poles by volunteers working at off-peak hours to "agitate driver peripheral perception and contribute to general road anxiety." The work was a "reaction to America's blissful ignorance to the dark future of Bush's nightmares."

Title: **Mom, We're Home!**
Format: **Poster**
Art Director/Designer:
John Yates
Client: **Stealworks**
Country: **USA**
Year: **1987**

This generic anti-war piece was designed to be used during the first Gulf War. It was later used by the Center for the Study of Political Graphics' art show "The Price of Intervention" in Los Angeles in 1991. A decade and a half later, the work feels equally poignant in regard to the fact that during the second Gulf War, the U.S. government censored photos of the returning dead, justifying this censorship as a matter of respect for the victims.

Title: **Casualties of War**
Format: **Poster**
Art Director/Designer:
Daniel Jasper
Client: **No client**
Country: **USA**
Year: **2004**

Tired of simplistic frothing at the mouth anti-Bush messages? This artist constructed his poster to withstand changes in both the environmental and political points of view. Using computer technology, the faces of individual soldiers who have lost their lives up to that point in the Iraq war have been used to construct George Bush's face, while the names of all the soldiers are listed around his image. In addition to the poster, the designer had tie tacks made of the flag draped coffin illustration *(top left corner)* as seen below.

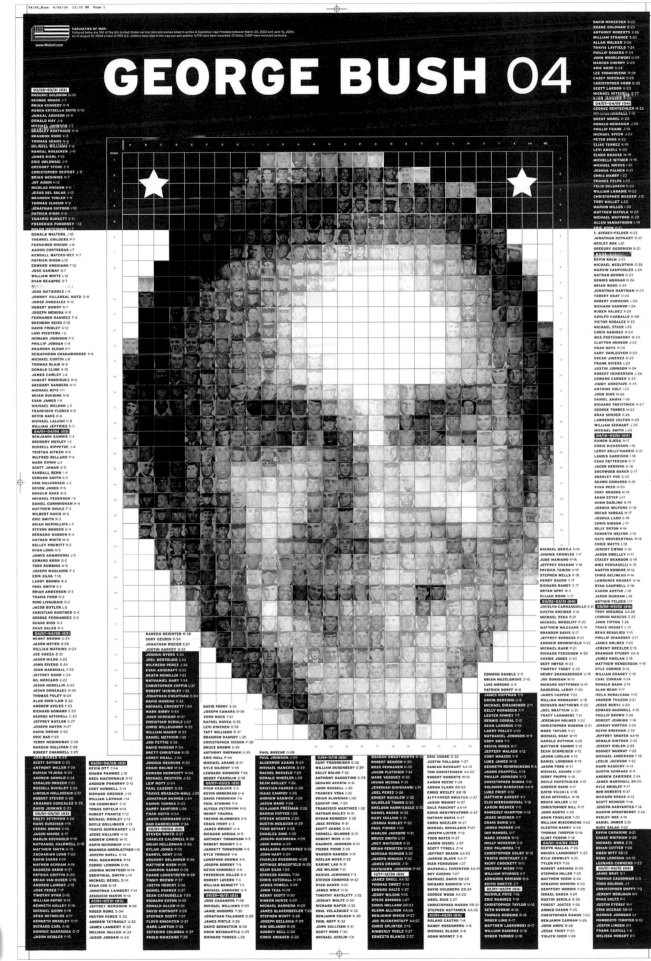

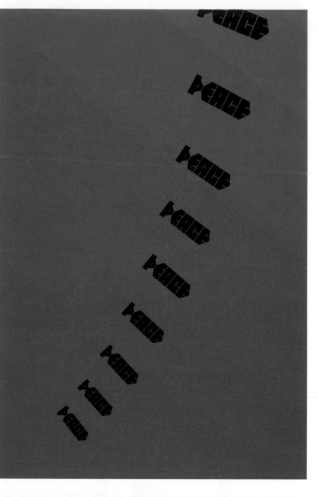

Title: Your Name Here
Format: **Poster**
Art Director/Designer:
Ellen Gould
Client:
AnotherPosterForPeace.org
Country: **USA**
Year: **2003**

Writing personal messages on bombs became a common practice during WWII. Here that space is offered for corporate advertising in this free, downloadable poster available on the Internet. *(top left)*

Title: Bombing Peace
Format: **Poster**
Art Director/Designer:
Samuli Viitasaari
Client: **No client**
Country: **Finland**
Year: **2003**

This poster, posted in and around Kuopio, Finland, contemplates how easily people adapt to and believe even the "harshest lies," as long as they are told to us by our leaders. The designer notes that it's almost as if there is a switch that can be flicked to turn off an entire nation's common sense, whereby aggression is suddenly seen as a sign of good-heartedness, while attempts to avoid violence make one a no-good traitor. *(top right)*

Title: NO War
Format: **New Year's greetings card**
Art Director/Designer:
Patrick Thomas
Client: **Studio la Vista**
Country: **Spain**
Year: **2002**

A 2003 New Year's greeting card in the form of a stencil gave recipients the tool to actively oppose the impending war in Iraq. *(middle & bottom)*

Title: **Places the U.S. Has Bombed Since World War Two**
Format: **Poster**
Art Director/Designer: **Josh MacPhee**
Client: **No client**
Country: **USA**
Year: **2002**

Falling bombs with the names of the countries the United States has bombed since World War II convey the scope and shocking impact of U.S. foreign policy since WWII.

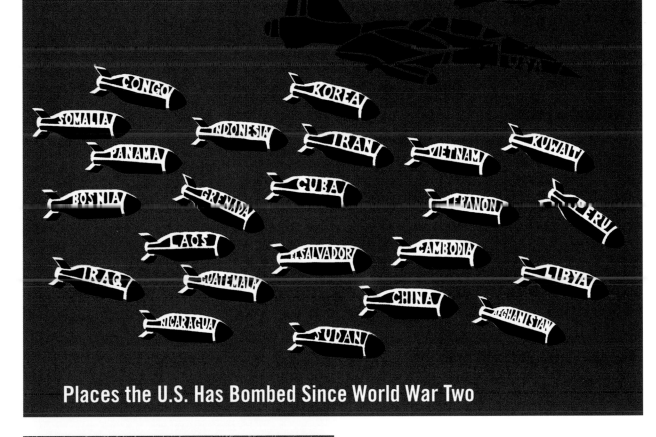

Places the U.S. Has Bombed Since World War Two

Title: **Endgame**
Format: **Poster**
Art Director/Designer: **Milton Glaser**
Client: **Lawyer's Committee on Nuclear Policy**
Country: **USA**
Year: **2004**

The word endgame was intended to have two meanings. The first refers to the fact that ignoring nuclear proliferation could lead to the end of life on earth. The second reflects the idea that it is time to end that threat altogether.

Title: **We Don't Need Another Hiro**
Format: **Poster**
Art Director/Designer:
Yossi Lemel
Client: **No client**
Country: **Israel**
Year: **2003**

This poster, which coincides with the fiftieth anniversary of the bombing of Hiroshima, is an expression of protest against France's decision to renew its nuclear testing on the Mururoa islands. Changing "Hero" to "Hiro" in this well-known musical lyric serves as a historical reminder of how easily good intentions can lead to tragedy.

Title: **Third War**
Format: **Poster**
Art Director/Designer:
Tahamtan Aminian
Client: **Fioreh Publication**
Country: **Iran**
Year: **2003**

The apples in this picture cleverly suggest a pregnant woman targeted by the possibility of a third world war and, as a result, the extinction of the human race.

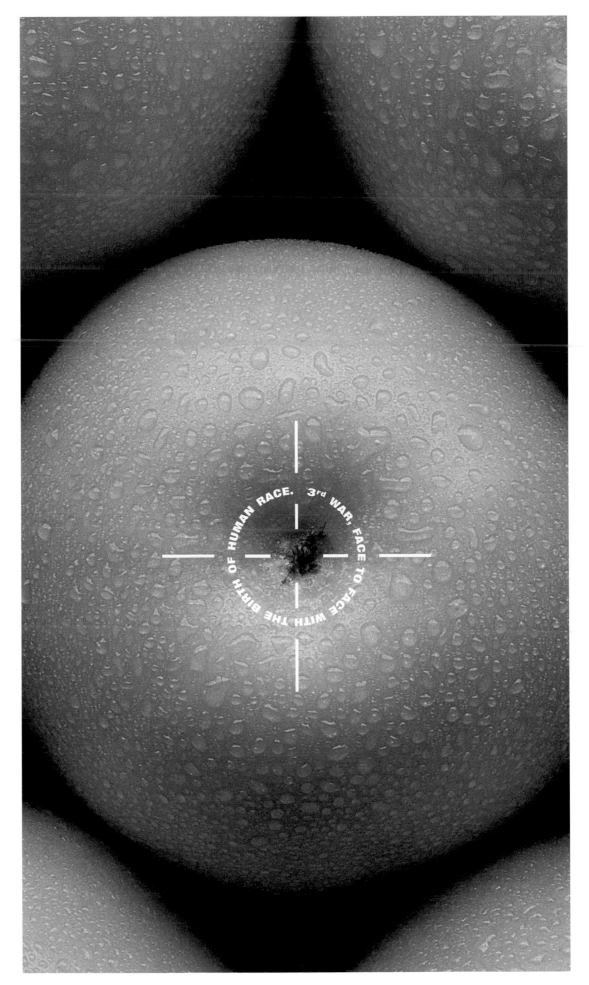

Title: WAR = DEATH
Format: Poster
Art Director/Designer:
Michael Mabry
Client:
AnotherPosterForPeace.org
Country: **USA**
Year: **2003**

This copyright-free poster was specifically designed for free downloads. Another Poster for Peace is an organization created in response to the Bush Administration's brilliant pro-war marketing. Design is used to support a grassroots anti-campaign: "If enough of us voice our dissent, we will be heard." *(top left)*

Title: WAR—I hate this game
Format: Antiwar sign
Art Director/Designer:
Jugoslav Vlahović
Client: *NIN* weekly newspaper
Country: **Serbia and Montenegro**
Year: **1999**

The NBA logo, which is well-known in Serbia and Montenegro because of their successful team, was appropriated to make this antiwar sign. The newly created logo was very popular in Yugoslavia, appearing on T-shirts, in magazines, and over the Internet during the NATO bombings in 1999. *(top right)*

Title: Pentagon: Bloody Red
Format: Poster
Art Director/Designer:
Alireza Mostafazadeh Ebrahimi
Client: **Negar**
Country: **Iran**
Year: **2004**

The creator of this poster uses a Pantone color chip, the most commonly used color matching system by design professionals, as a way of representing America's war policies, and suggesting that "Bloody Red" may be the only color the Pentagon knows. *(bottom)*

MAKE UP, NOT WAR

Thea Line cosmetics

Title: **Make Up, Not War**
Format: **Cosmetics ad**
Art Director/Designer:
Igor Avzner
Client: **Thea Line
cosmetics**
Country: **Serbia and
Montenegro**
Year: **Unknown**

This antiwar advertisement,
produced by a cosmetics
company in Serbia, replaced
bullets in a cartridge belt
with lipstick. It was used by
militia to convey its hope
for peace.

Title: **Burnt**
Format: **Holiday card**
Art Director/Designer:
Lisa Gibson
Client: **No client**
Country: **USA**
Year: **2003**

During a season of warm
wishes and good cheer, it is
especially poignant to
receive a holiday card
focused on how peace, the
most vital thread keeping
our world united and
healthy, has been burned
and broken.

better luck next year

Peace on Earth

Title: **The Iran for Land Peace**
Format: **Poster**
Art Director/Designer: **Mehdi Saeedi**
Client: **Sepah**
Country: **Iran**
Year: **Unknown**

The words Iran Land of Peace are repeated in different sizes to construct a nest for this fragile bird.

Title: **Peace**
Format: **Electronic poster**
Art Director/Designer: **Mr. Tharp (inspired by Sam Smidt)**
Client: **AnotherPosterForPeace.org**
Country: **USA**
Year: **2003**

This downloadable electronic image was designed for AnotherPosterForPeace.org, an online source for copyright-free images promoting peace.

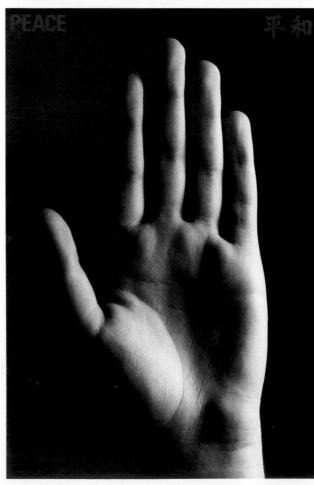

Title: **King Kong & Godzilla**
Format: **Poster**
Art Director/Designer:
Steff Geissbuhler
Client:
Shoshin Society (Japan)
Country: **USA**
Year: **1985**

U.S. designers were asked to create and contribute a poster to commemorate the bombing of Hiroshima. This poster encouraged reconciliation between the two giants (the US and the USSR symbolized by Godzilla and King Kong) that could destroy the world. It was part of the Images for Survival traveling exhibition and book as a gift to the Museum of Modern Art in Hiroshima, Japan. *(top left)*

Title: **A Fragile World**
Format: **Poster**
Art Director/Designer:
Ivan Chermayeff
Client:
Shoshin Society (Japan)
Country: **USA**
Year: **1985**

A classic idyllic image on an antique plate has been shattered. The plate, crudely taped back together, demonstrates the fragility of life and our world and how difficult it is to put things right again after they have gone wrong. *(top right)*

Title: **My Daughter's Hand**
Format: **Poster**
Art Director/Designer:
Tom Geismar
Client:
Shoshin Society (Japan)
Country: **USA**
Year: **1985**

This image of the designer's daughter's hand conveys both the idea of "peace" and "stop." The intrinsic lines and creases of the open palm also suggest the uniqueness and sanctity of each individual life. *(bottom)*

Title: **Victory**
Format: **Poster**
Art Director/Designer:
Fang Chen
Client: **No client**
Country: **USA**
Year: **1998**

This artist writes of his work, "The capitalized V represented by the two fingers is a universal symbol for victory and is understood by viewers of all races and cultures. According to Chinese folklore, the lines in human hands are not only records of the past but also foretell the future." In his work, these lines and the missing fingers also speak to the reality that human beings often experience suffering in order to achieve triumph

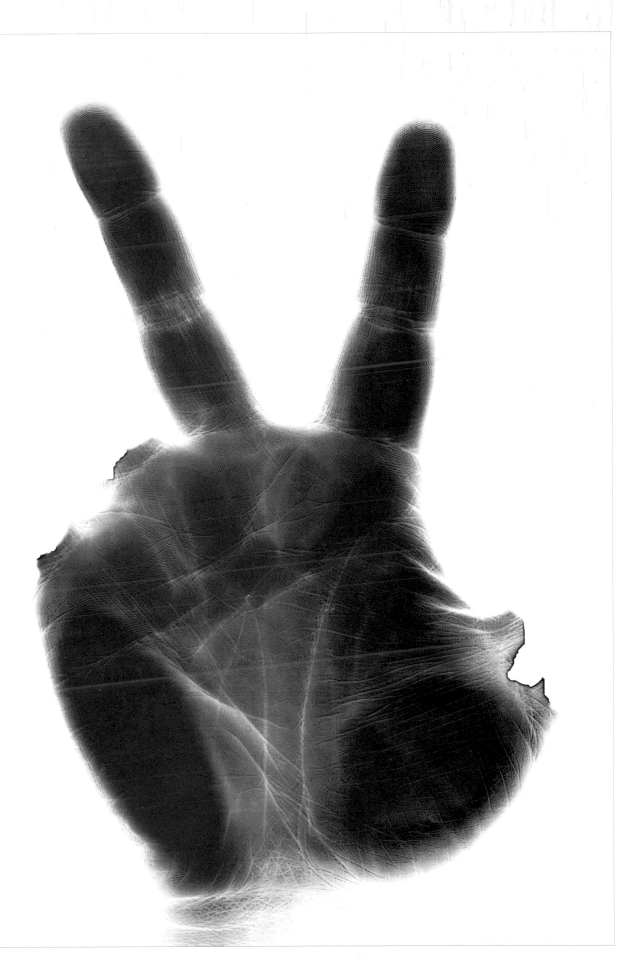

Title: **Racism**
Format: **Poster**
Art Director/Designer:
Cedomir Kostović
Client: **Southwest
Missouri State University**
Country: **USA**
Year: **1998**

Simple, poignant, and
powerful, this image
effectively illustrates the
irrationality of racism.

Title: howiloveya
Format: **Poster**
Art Director/Designer:
Mark Fox
Client: **BlackDog**
Country: **USA**
Year: **1998**

This poster argues that Mickey Mouse is a racist figure based on a blackface character.

Title: **Use Wyten to Cover-up**
Format: **Magazine spread**
Art Director/Designers:
**Garth Walker,
Brandt Botes**
Client: *I-Jusi* **magazine**
Country: **South Africa**
Year: **1999**

I-Jusi (juice in Zulu) is a free graphic design magazine published in Durban, South Africa. This image was created for "The Black & White" issue and is a comment on an apartheid era concept of black-skinned people wanting to appear more white. Skin lighteners, which are proven to be damaging to the skin, are still employed by many non-whites.

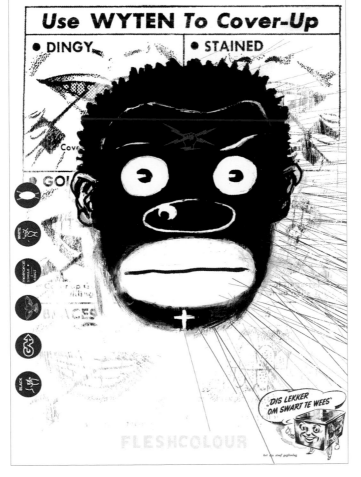

Title: **Laudium Welcomes Comrade Mandela**
Format: **Poster**
Art Director/Designer: **Unknown**
Client: **Unknown**
Country: **South Africa**
Year: **1990**

This poster welcoming Mandela for his visit to the township Laudium, and the ones to the right, were produced in the "old South Africa" and was therefore illegal under the terms of the "state of emergency." Posters of this nature are now virtually impossible to come by.

Title: **Happy Birthday
Nelson Mandela**
Format: **Poster**
Art Director/Designer:
Unknown
Client: **Mandela Birthday
Committee, Cape Town**
Country: **South Africa**
Year: **1988**

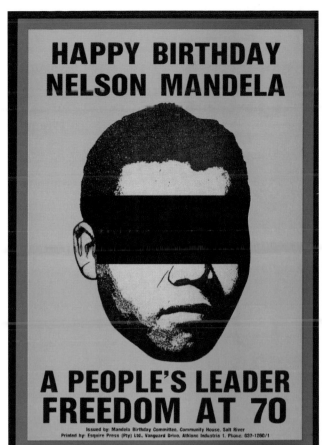

Title: **Release Nelson
Mandela**
Format: **Poster**
Art Director/Designer:
Surinder Singh
Client: **Anti-Apartheid
Movement**
Country: **South Africa**
Year: **1988**

These Anti-Apartheid
posters from the 1980s
demanded freedom for
Nelson Mandela and also
wished him a "happy
70th birthday" in prison.
The government ban on
Nelson Mandela's physical
image contributed to the
absence of compelling
current photographs.
(top right)

Title: **Make-up
for Beginners**
Format: **Poster**
Art Director/Designer:
Joost Veerkamp
Client: **Stichting Culture
in Another South Africa,
Amsterdam**
Country: **South Africa**
Year: **1987**

Pieter Willem Botha, the
president of South Africa
from 1984 to 1989, was
forced to resign by his own
party and was succeded by
Frederik W. de Klerk who
ultimately dismantled the
apartheid system, holding
free and fair elections. Here
we see him being forcefully
changed into Nelson
Mandela. *(bottom)*

Title: **Article 4**
Article 15/Article 29
Format: **Poster**
Art Director/Designer:
Chaz Maviyane-Davies
Client: **No client**
Country: **USA**
Year: **1996**

These pieces were part of a series of thirteen posters based on the United Nations Articles on Human Rights as seen from the African perspective.

Article

Rights 4

No one should be subjected to slavery or servitude

QUANTEL

todos los hombres somos iguales?

IGNORANCIA = INTOLERANCIA   un mundo feliz / a happy world production

Title: **Todos Los Hombres Somos Iguales?**
Format: **Poster**
Art Director/Designers: **Sonia Freeman, Gabriel Freeman**
Client: **Un Mundo Feliz/A Happy World Production**
Country: **Spain**

Part of the Ignorance = Intolerance project and inspired by the fiftieth anniversary of the Declaration of Human Rights, in 1998, this poster attempts to redefine conventional concepts of equality.

Title: **Poster Against Xenophoby**
Format: **Poster**
Art Director/Designers:
**Sonia Freeman,
Gabriel Freeman**
Client: **Istituto Europeo di Design**
Country: **Spain**
Year: **2002**

The handprint illustrates the stupidity of xenophobia in a world made up of mixed blood. The poster was created for a themed exhibition on "half-bred people" at the IED (Istituto Europeo di Design) in Madrid. (*top left*)

Title: **Poster Against Torture**
Format: **Poster**
Art Director/Designers:
**Sonia Freeman,
Gabriel Freeman**
Client: **Un Mundo Feliz/A Happy World Production**
Country: **Spain**
Year: **2001**

The clean, simple style of this illustration reinforces the message that torture is not confined to any particular political system; it occurs in democracies as well as dictatorships and under civilian, as well as military governments. The work was distributed free over the Internet. (*top right*)

Title: **Bolted Hands**
Format: **Poster**
Art Director/Designer:
Lanny Sommese
Client: **Amnesty International chapter at Penn State University**
Country: **USA**
Year: **1981**

This dynamic poster for Amnesty International was designed to raise awareness about the torture that humans continually inflict upon one another and to remind viewers of Amnesty's mission. The visceral drip drawing style of the praying hands was used to contrast the mechanically drawn bolt and heighten the emotional impact of the image. The bolt and hands were then scaled and juxtaposed to appear as a cross "to make the image more emblematic." (*bottom*)

Title: **Tout les homes sont égaux**
Format: **Poster**
Art Director/Designer:
Ebrahim Haghighi
Client: **No client**
Country: **Iran**
Year: **2003**

Totalitarianism inevitably produces cynicism and despair. This work proclaims "all men are equal" yet begets the observation that such equality only occurs after death.

THE **AMERICAN**™ **DREAM**

DEVIL MAY CARE

Title: **Devil May Care**
Format: **Poster**
Art Director/Designer:
Jeff Louviere
Client: **The American™ Dream**
Country: **USA**
Year: **2002**

The consequences of the laissez-faire spirit of New Orleans is revealed by an image of legendary stunt man, Evil Knievel moto-vaulting over a long line of degraded and exploited dark skinned men. The designer created this poster in response to the lack of social commentary in New Orleans, and posted them around the city in the middle of the night.

Title: **Migranti
Diritti e Pace**
Format: **Poster**
Art Director/Designer:
Mauro Bubbico
Client: **Social
Forum Matera**
Country: **Italy**
Year: **Unknown**

The dark-skinned model
holds a target to make clear
the xenophobic racist
consequences on
immigrants on this poster
protesting a new
discriminatory Italian
immigration law.

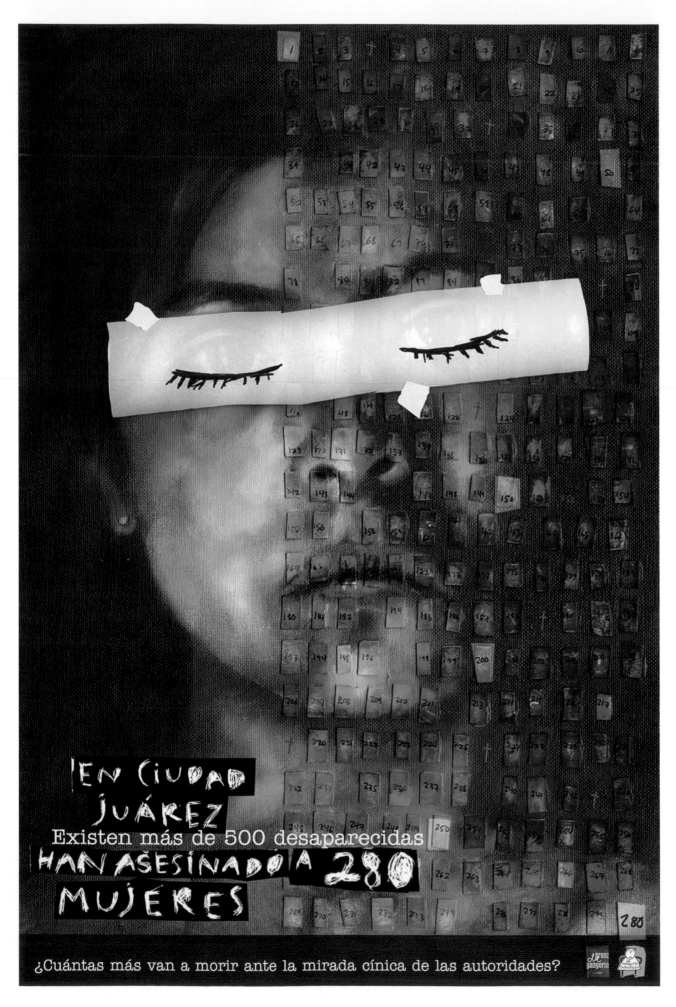

Title: **More Than 280 Women Have Been Murdered**
Format: **Poster**
Art Director/Designer: **Margarita Sada**
Client: **Die Gresgangerin**
Country: **Mexico**
Year: **2002**

The designer notes "For more than ten years, hundreds of women in the Mexican town of Juarez have been kidnapped, raped, murdered, and grotesquely maimed. After years of official apathy and police incompetence toward solving and ending these brutal murders, the families of the missing women started actions to demand justice. I made this poster to support their stuggle." The text reads "More than 280 women have been murdered in Juárez City and another 500 more are missing. How many more are going to die under the cynical stare of authorities?"

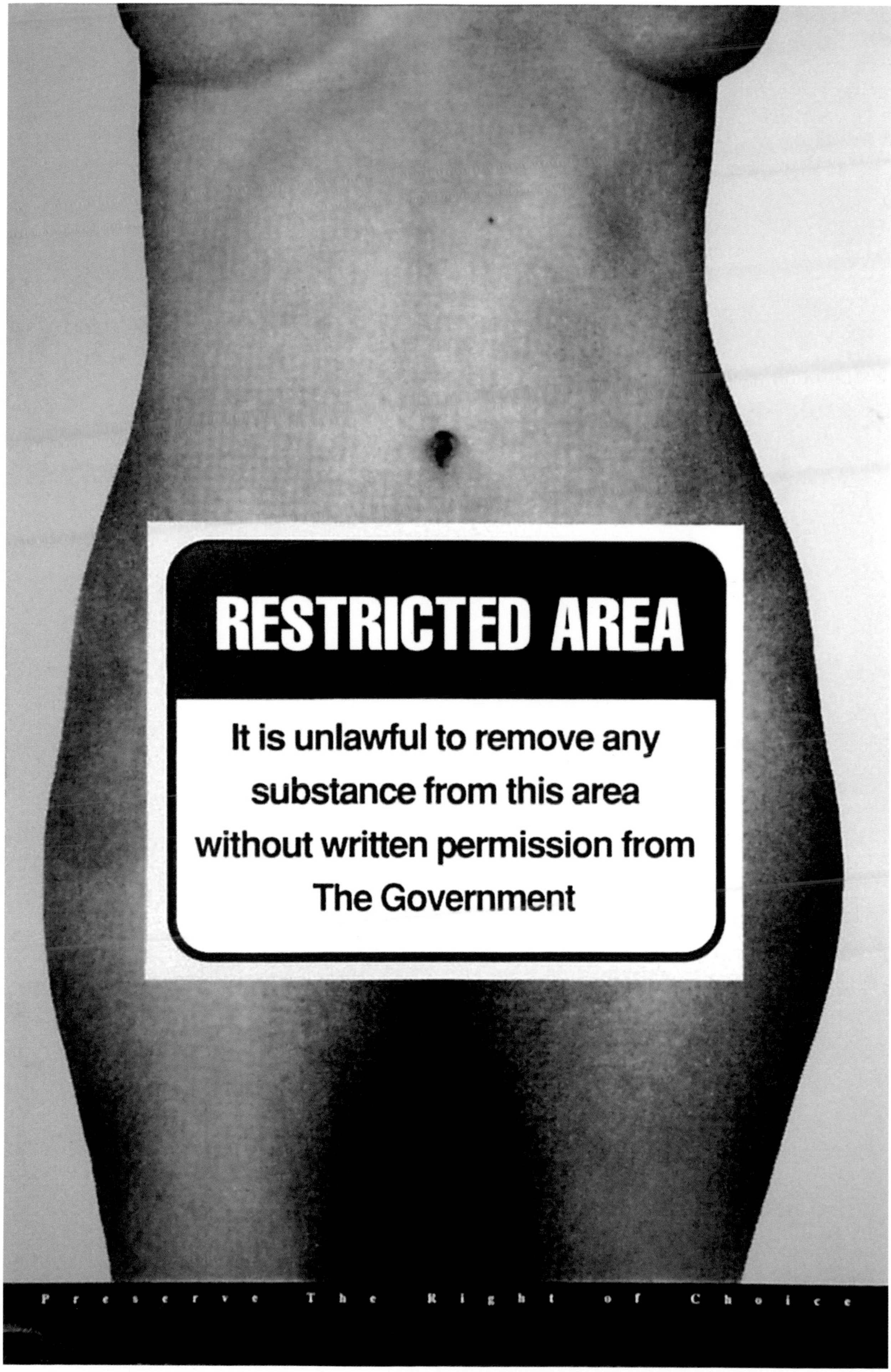

Title: **Preserve the
Right of Choice**
Format: **Poster**
Art Director/Designer:
Trudy Cole-Zielanski
Client: **No client**
Country: **USA**
Year: **1993**

"This poster was designed to
promote the understanding
that a woman's body is her
own, and she has the
ultimate right to say what
she does with it."

RESTRICTED AREA

It is unlawful to remove any substance from this area without written permission from The Government

Preserve The Right of Choice

IT'S ABOUT TIME

BenchMark
NCJW's Campaign to Save Roe

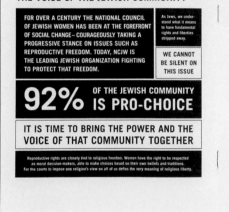

NCJW'S VOICE:
THE VOICE OF THE JEWISH COMMUNITY

FOR OVER A CENTURY THE NATIONAL COUNCIL OF JEWISH WOMEN HAS BEEN AT THE FOREFRONT OF SOCIAL CHANGE—COURAGEOUSLY TAKING A PROGRESSIVE STANCE ON ISSUES SUCH AS REPRODUCTIVE FREEDOM. TODAY, NCJW IS THE LEADING JEWISH ORGANIZATION FIGHTING TO PROTECT THAT FREEDOM.

As Jews, we understand what it means to have fundamental rights and liberties stripped away.

WE CANNOT BE SILENT ON THIS ISSUE

92% OF THE JEWISH COMMUNITY IS PRO-CHOICE

IT IS TIME TO BRING THE POWER AND THE VOICE OF THAT COMMUNITY TOGETHER

Reproductive rights are closely tied to religious freedom. Women have the right to be respected as moral decision-makers, able to make choices based on their own beliefs and traditions. For the courts to impose one religion's view on all of us defies the very meaning of religious liberty.

NCJW'S BENCHMARK CAMPAIGN IS ALREADY TAKING ACTION:

EDUCATING AND MOBILIZING THOUSANDS OF PEOPLE

LEADING PRO-CHOICE RALLIES AND COMMUNITY EVENTS ACROSS THE COUNTRY

BUILDING STATE COALITIONS

FLYING KEY LEADERS AND SPEAKERS TO WASHINGTON, DC TO MEET WITH SENATORS

EMPOWERING ONLINE ACTIVISTS VIA ALERTS, UPDATES, AND AN INTERACTIVE WEB SITE

NOW, IT'S YOUR TURN

LOG ON TO WWW.BENCHMARKCAMPAIGN.ORG AND JOIN BENCHMARK TODAY

BENCHMARK, THE NATIONAL COUNCIL OF JEWISH WOMEN'S CAMPAIGN TO SAVE ROE EDUCATES, MOBILIZES, AND ADVOCATES— REACHING OUT TO THE DECISION-MAKERS IN WASHINGTON, DC TO DELIVER YOUR VOICE ON THE IMPORTANCE OF FUNDAMENTAL FREEDOMS, INCLUDING WOMEN'S RIGHT TO REPRODUCTIVE CHOICE.

The right to make independent childbearing decisions has enabled women to pursue educational and employment opportunities that were unthinkable a generation ago.

Title: **It's About Time**
Format: **Brochure**
Art Director/Designers:
**David Schimmel,
Susan Brzozowski**
Client: **National Council
of Jewish Women**
Country: **USA**
Year: **2004**

Serving as both a wake up call and a call to action, this booklet informs readers of the threats facing Roe vs. Wade and urges them to protect their right to safe, legal abortion by contacting their senators.

Title: **I'mmoral**
Format: **Poster**
Art Director/Designers:
**AddisGroup–John
Creson, Monica Schlaug**
Client: **Planned
Parenthood**
Country: **USA**
Year: **2004**

For this poster announcing the "Reframing the Argument for Reproductive Choice" gala, an apostrophe was added to change the meaning of the tattooed word immoral to "I'm moral." The image also evokes *The Scarlet Letter* and the pain felt by a stigmatized woman.

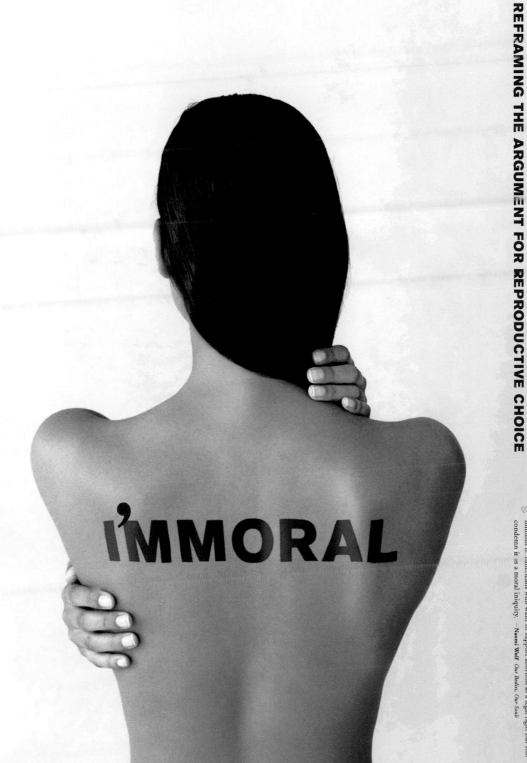

PLANNED PARENTHOOD GOLDEN GATE GALA 2004

REFRAMING THE ARGUMENT FOR REPRODUCTIVE CHOICE

"By refusing to look at abortion within a moral framework, we lose the millions of Americans who want to support abortion as a legal right but still condemn it as a moral iniquity. —**Naomi Wolf** *Our Bodies, Our Souls*

Title: **Ethiopia Planned Parenthood**
Format: **Poster**
Art Director/Designers: **Nancy Hoefig, Monica Schlang**
Client: **Planned Parenthood**
Country: **USA**
Year: **2001**

An alliance between Planned Parenthood and its Ethiopian counterpart neatly refers to the goal of successful birth control access by cleverly using various types of contraception to construct an African-inspired mask for a gala invitation.

Title: **Price of Life**
Format: **Poster**
Art Director/Designer:
Wishmini Perera
Client: **No client**
Country: **USA**
Year: **2003**

In this poster, done for a class assignment, traditional bridal decorations are used to oppose the dowry system practiced in South Asia. The hand is held up as if to say "Stop!"

Title: **Sri Lanka**
Format: **Postcard**
Art Director/Designer:
Chaz Maviyane-Davies
Client: **No client**
Country: **USA**
Year: **2002**

This is a commentary on former Sri Lankan Prime Minister Ratnasiri Wickremanayake's speech in which he urged the country to support war efforts by having more babies to swell the ranks of the army and vanquish separatist Tamil Tiger rebels.

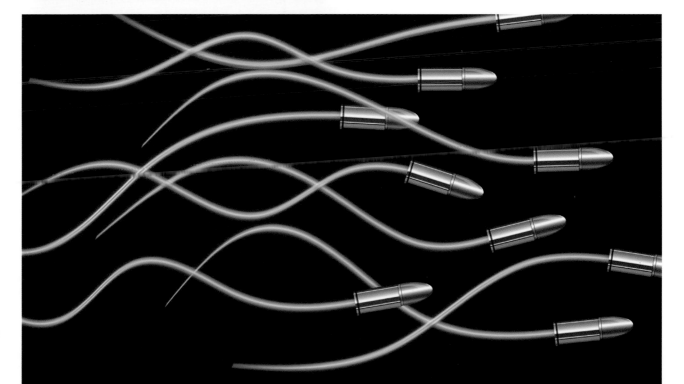

Title: **Crucified Woman**
Format: **Illustration**
Illustrator: **Eric Drooker**
Client: *The Village Voice*
Country: **USA**
Year: **1991**

This image of a woman, prosecuted through the centuries by the hands of governments and religious leaders, has become a popular icon and tattoo design among feminists internationally. (*top left*)

Title: **Freedom for Women Political Prisoners**
Format: **Poster**
Art Director/Designer: **Margarita Sada**
Client: **No client**
Country: **Mexico**
Year: **1999**

In 1999, the students of the National University in Mexico City went on strike to demand the democratization of political institutions. The strike lasted ten months, ending when the police broke in and imprisoned hundreds of students, many of whom were girls. The text reads: "Freedom for Women Political Prisoners. March 8th International Day of Women. Lots of Girls. We are bad and we can be worse." (*top right*)

Title: **Republicans Against Choice**
Format: **Illustration**
Illustrator: **Frances Jetter**
Client: **Davidson Galleries**
Country: **USA**
Year: **1992**

The similarity between the appearance of an elephant (Republican symbol) head and a woman's reproductive organs was used to comment on the republican party's position on abortion. Originally commissioned and then refused by the *New York Times* op-ed pages, it was eventually published by *The Village Voice* and then printed on T-shirts. (*bottom*)

Title: **Sex and the Supreme Court**
Format: **Poster**
Art Director/Designer: **Joanne Hom**
Client: **Planned Parenthood**
Country: **USA**
Year: **2003**

This ominous reference to coat-hanger abortions is used as an effective graphic warning on an invitation to a Planned Parenthood fundraiser.

Title: **Class Action**
Format: **T-shirts**
Art Director/Designers: **Rodney Abbot, Debra Drovillo, Lisa Mangano, Alexandra Min, Louise Scovell, Lisa Shoglow**
Client: **No client**
Country: **USA**
Year: **1992**

A small collective of graduate students at Yale joined forces to raise awareness of the issue of protecting a woman's right to choose. This T-shirt illustrates the conflict between those who believe that abortion is an individual decision as protected by the Roe v. Wade decision and those who feel it is something that should be decided by government.

Title: **Class Action**
Format: **Billboard**
Art Director/Designers:
**Rodney Abbot,
Debra Drovillo,
Lisa Mangano,
Alexandra Min,
Louise Scovell,
Lisa Shoglow**
Client: **No client**
Country: **USA**
Year: **1992**

This pro-choice message was produced as a billboard situated prominently on the highly trafficked route I-95 in Connecticut.

Title: **The Anatomically Correct Oscar**
Format: **Billboard**
Art Director/Designer:
Guerilla Girls, Inc.
Client: **No client**
Country: **USA**
Year: **2001**

"The anatomically correct Oscar: He's white & male, just like the guys who win!" This billboard, sponsored by the Guerilla Girls, was displayed a few blocks away from the Academy Awards ceremony to point out the sexism and racism that's rampant in the film industry.

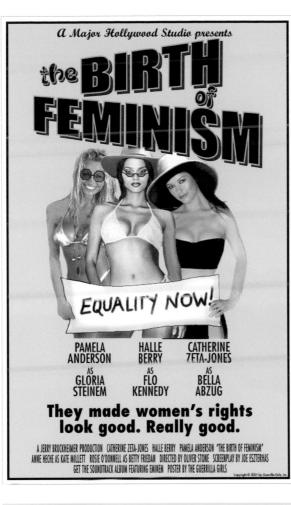

Title: The Birth
of Feminism
Format: Poster
Art Director/Designer:
Guerrilla Girls, Inc.
Client: No client
Country: USA
Year: 2001

This parody of a major
Hollywood studio poster
features well-known
actresses portraying three
of the most important U.S.
feminist activists of recent
times in their signature
looks. Pink sunglasses and a
cowboy hat were Kennedy's
trademarks, Abzug favored
dramatic headwear, and
Steinem is known for her
large glasses.

Title: Do Women Have
to Be Naked to Get
Into the Met. Museum?
Format: Poster
Art Director/Designer:
Guerilla Girls, Inc.
Client: No client
Country: USA
Year: 1989

Since 1985, the Guerrilla
Girls, a bunch of
anonymous females
who take the names of
dead women artists as
pseudonyms and appear in
public wearing gorilla
masks, have produced more
than one hundred posters,
stickers, books, printed
projects, and actions that
expose sexism and racism
in politics, the art world,
film, and the culture at
large. This poster protests
the lack of female artists in
the Metropolitan Museum
of Art and questions "Do
women have to be naked to
get into the Met Museum?"

Title: **Musical Expressions**
Format: **Poster series**
Art Director/Designers:
**Tan Kien Eng,
Theresa Tsang Teng**
Client: **Women's Aid
Organization (WAO)**
Country: **Malaysia**
Year: **Unknown**

A series of posters
promoting a benefit concert
whose proceeds went to
Women's Aid Organization
to help fight gender
violence.

DON'T wear make-up.

Don't wear your hair long.

Don't wear short skirts.

Don't wear high heels.

Don't wear tight-fitting clothes.

Don't look sexy.

Don't bat your eyelashes.

Don't crack dirty jokes.

Don't flirt.

Don't smile at strangers.

Don't offer help to strangers.

Don't go out at night.

Don't go to parties.

Don't go on dates.

Don't go anywhere alone.

Don't attract attention.

Don't work late.

Don't trust anyone.

Don't say yes.

Don't say no.

Don't be a woman.

Don't exist.

Do call Women's Aid Organisation at 03-7956 3488 to help stop prejudice and violence against women. You can make a difference.

Title: **Don't**
Format: **Poster**
Art Director/Designer:
Tan Kien Eng
Client: **Women's Aid Organization (WAO)**
Country: **Malaysia**
Year: **Unknown**

This poster rebuffs a campaign to discourage violence against Malaysian women by urging modesty. Here, the designer opposes this concept through irony and the punch line "don't exist."

Title: **Front Page**
Format: **Flipbook**
Art Director/Designer:
Dušan Petričić
Client:
Galleria Graficki Kolektiv
Country: **Yugoslavia**
Year: **1971**

This privately published catalogue-flipbook from Communist Yugoslavia shows the human need for freedom and self-expression. (*far right and following pages*)

Title: **Search and Destroy**
Format: **Magazine cover**
Art Director/Designer:
Scott Stowell
Client: *The Nation*
Country: **USA**
Year: **2000**

This cover addresses the U.S. military's intolerance of homosexuality and their "don't ask, don't tell" policy by covering the classic ACT UP "silence = death" pink triangle with camouflage.

Title: **Gay Teen Suicide**
Format: **Poster**
Art Director/Designers:
**Sean Adams,
Ashton Taylor**
Photographer: **Blake Little**
Client: **World Studio
Foundation**
Country: **USA**
Year: **2003**

This poster was designed to promote awareness of the disproportionally high occurrence of suicide among gay teenagers.

NEW PALTZ • NEW YORK • 2004

I DO!

SUPPORT SAME-SEX MARRIAGE, MAYOR JASON WEST, REVEREND KAY GREENLEAF & REVEREND DAWN SANGREY

DESIGN: JEFF FISHER LOGOMOTIVES © 2004

Title: I DO!
Format: **Poster**
Art Director/Designer:
Jeff Fisher
Client: **No client**
Country: **USA**
Year: **2004**

After a public backlash to same-sex marriage licenses being issued in Multnomah County, Oregon, this designer created the "I DO!" image and distributed it via email for use by those supporting the legalization of same-sex marriage. Flyers, stickers, and buttons were produced and displayed in the windows of businesses and homes, on the bumpers of cars, and at public hearings on the topic. Similar items were also designed for campaigns in California, Massachusetts, New York, and New Mexico.

Title: **LGBT Marriage and Family**
Format: **Brochure**
Art Director/Designer:
Mirko Ilić
Client: **MLGBA (Massachusetts Lesbian and Gay Bar Association)**
Country: **USA**
Year: **2004**

This illustration originally appeared in the *Village Voice*, a New York free newspaper, accompanying a story on gay marriage. It caught the eye of the Massachusetts Lesbian and Gay Bar Association, who now use it on the covers of their informational brochures that outline how marriage will affect individual's rights and benefits. The image was inspired by the famous picture *V-J Day, The Kiss*, taken in 1945 by Alfred Eisenstaedt, in which a sailor is kissing a nurse in Times Square on Victory in Japan Day.

Title: **AIDS!**
Format: **Poster**
Art Director/Designer:
Fang Chen
Client: **No client**
Country: **USA**
Year: **2003**

The war against AIDS is literally depicted in this poster promoting awareness. The helmet, used as a visual metaphor, reminds us that war has its casualties but perhaps this image's strength lies in its deliberate provocation to discuss a subject too often ignored.

Old Glory condoms and T-shirts, for ordering information call
1-800-726-1930
in Massachusetts call 508-487-1930
10 A.M. - 4 P.M. E.S.T., Mon.-Fri.
order form enclosed

Old Glory Pledge

We believe it is patriotic to protect and save lives. We offer only the highest quality condoms. Join us in promoting safer sex. Help eliminate AIDS.

A portion of Old Glory profits will be donated to AIDS related services.

Old Glory Condom Corporation
Provincetown, MA 02657
Made in U.S.A.

This product combines a latex condom and a spermicidal lubricant. The spermicide nonoxynol-9 reduces the number of active sperm thereby decreasing the risk of pregnancy if you lose your erection before withdrawal and some semen spill outside the condom. However, the extent of decreased risk has not been established. This condom should not be used as a substitute for the combined use of a vaginal spermicide and a condom.

Title: **Old Glory Condoms**
Format: **Condom packaging**
Art Director/Designers:
Judy Kohn,
Kohn Kruikshank
Client: **Old Glory Condom Corp.**
Country: **USA**
Year: **1989**

In 1989, the government was challenged to redefine patriotism after the Supreme Court decision protecting flag-burning under the First Amendment was enacted. The U.S. Department of Commerce refused a trademark, during the height of the AIDS epidemic, saying it was "immoral and scandalous" to associate the flag with sex. Three years later, the name and image were finally granted trademark protections.

NON FARTI
SORPRENDERE
DALL'AIDS
COPRITI

Title: **Copriti**
Format: **Poster**
Art Director/Designer:
Mauro Bubbico
Client: **AIAP**
Country: **Italy**
Year: **Unknown**

This poster asks viewers to
"cover-up" so as not to be
surprised by AIDS.

Human Resources are limited. What should be done with it, to live or to fight?

Title: **Human Resources**
Format: **Poster**
Art Director/Designer:
Tahamtan Aminian
Client: **Fioreh Publication**
Country: **Iran**
Year: **2002**

Gunnysacks can be employed to hold flour, used in creating life-sustaining bread, or as sandbags, used to erect the trenches of war. This poster acknowledges that we have limited resources and asks if we will use them "to live or to fight."

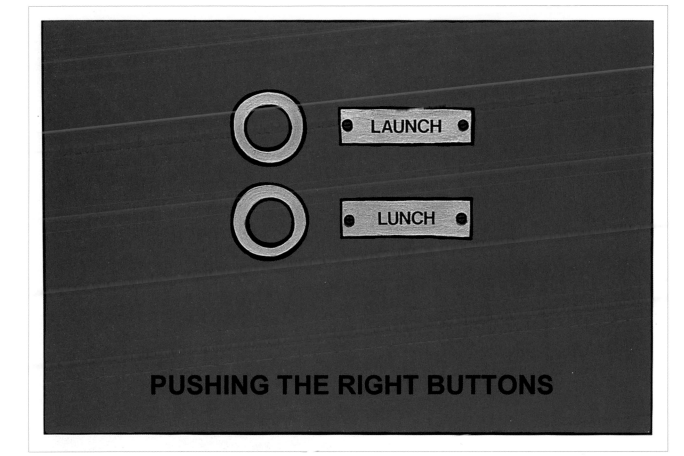

Title: **Pushing
the Right Buttons**
Format: **Illustration**
Art Director/Designer:
Erika Rothenberg
Client: **No client**
Country: **USA**
Year: **1982**

The political choice
between feeding the
hungry or military
aggression is dramatized
in this poster.

Title: **Over 17,000,000
Ukrainians Are Living
Below the Poverty Line**
Format: **Poster**
Art Director/Designer:
Anatoliy Omelchenko
Client: **Private Bank**
Country: **USA**
Year: **2000**

The text reading "Over
17,000,000 Ukrainians
Are Living Below the
Poverty Line" is simply and
effectively illustrated with
the familiar graphic
admonishment to properly
dispose of trash. Items
casually discarding by one
are all too often desperately
searched for by another, in
an effort to survive.

Понад 17,000,000 українців живуть за межею бідності.

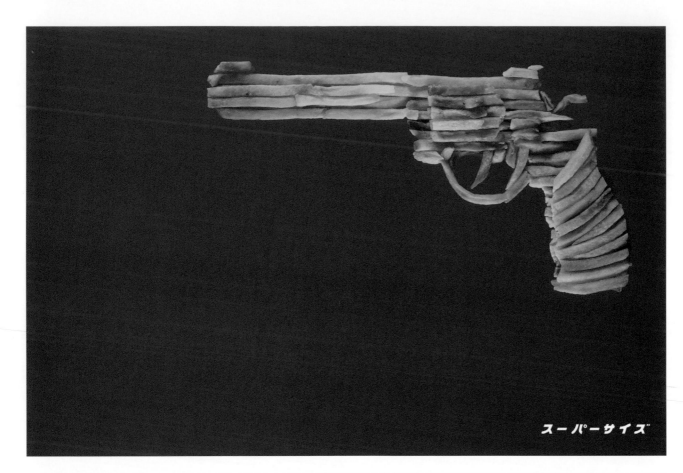

スーパーサイズ

Title: **Supersize**
Format: **Magazine spread**
Creative Directors:
**Joshua Berger,
Niko Courtelis,
Pete McCracken,
Enrique Mosqueda**
Art Director/Designers:
**Niko Courtelis,
Enrique Mosqueda**
Photographer:
Dan Forbes
Client: *IDEA*
magazine (Japan)
Country: **USA**
Year: **2000**

These images were created
for the Japanese design
magazine *IDEA* for a
special issue entitled
"Made in America." The
inherent health risks in
consuming fast food,
America's most visible and
influential export, is clearly
communicated in these
simple yet powerful images.

SUPERSIZE

Title: GMO Good Food
Format: Brochure
Art Director/Designer:
Jarek Bujny
Client: No client
Country: Poland
Year: 2004

They don't call genetically modified food "Frankenfood" for nothing! The hairs sprouting out of this otherwise lovely looking lemon creates a repulsive image that warns of the unknown dangers we face when playing with Mother Nature.

Title: Got Mad Cow?
Format: Poster
Art Director/Designer:
Sharon DiGiacinto
Client: No client
Country: USA
Year: 2004

This poster, parodying the very popular "Got Milk" campaign and a popular childhood rhyme, points out the ironic link between feeding cows (which are herbivores) ground-up body parts of animals and the creation of mad cow disease. In 2003, more than 36,800,000 cows were slaughtered, yet only 20,453 were tested. This frightening ratio indicates a significant disregard for public safety and the care of animals.

Title: *Dead Meat*
Format: **Book**
Designer/Illustrator:
Sue Coe
Client: **Four Walls
Eight Windows**
Country: **USA**
Year: **1995**

Sue Coe, fine artist, illustrator, and activist whose work appears on street corners as well as at the Metropolitan Museum of Art, is a dedicated animal rights advocate. She found a way to get herself inside slaughterhouses in America to create these powerful images documenting the cruelty and abuse animals experience in factory farming.

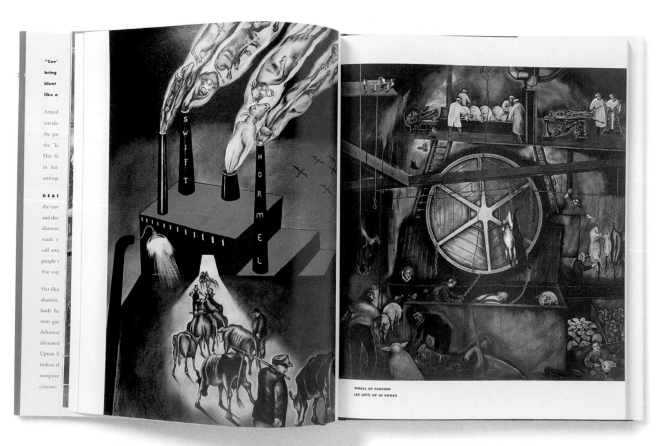

WHEEL OF FORTUNE
(AT LEFT) UP IN SMOKE

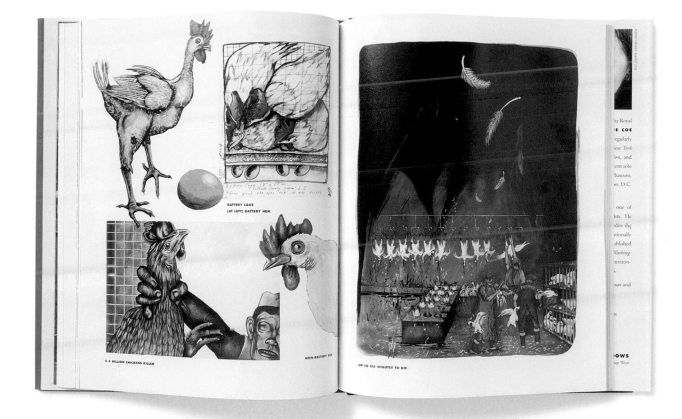

BATTERY CAGE
(AT LEFT) BATTERY HEN

5.5 BILLION CHICKENS KILLED

NON-BATTERY HEN

UP TO SIX MINUTES TO DIE

MEAT FLIES

END FACTORY FARMING   DON'T EAT MEAT   1.888.FARM.USA
FARMUSA.ORG   FARM

Title: **Dinner**
Format: **Poster series**
Art Director/Designer:
Sandra Scher
Client: **FARM**
Country: **USA**
Year: **2003**

END FACTORY FARMING   DON'T EAT MEAT   1.888.FARM.USA
FARMUSA.ORG   FARM

The harsh images of factory farming are difficult to bear. The animal rights organization FARM wanted to convince people not to eat meat by illustrating the cruel realities of factory farming with images of dead animals taking the place of a dinner plate. The silverware is arranged in a place setting to amplify the consequences of one's seemingly inconsequential choice.

Title: **What's Fer Dinner?**
Format: **Cards**
Art Director/Designer:
Kevin Grady
Client: **No client**
Country: **USA**
Year: **2001**

A set of twelve cards, juxtaposing photographs taken in a slaughterhouse with homey, old-fashioned recipes, provides an unnerving and powerful message protesting factory farming

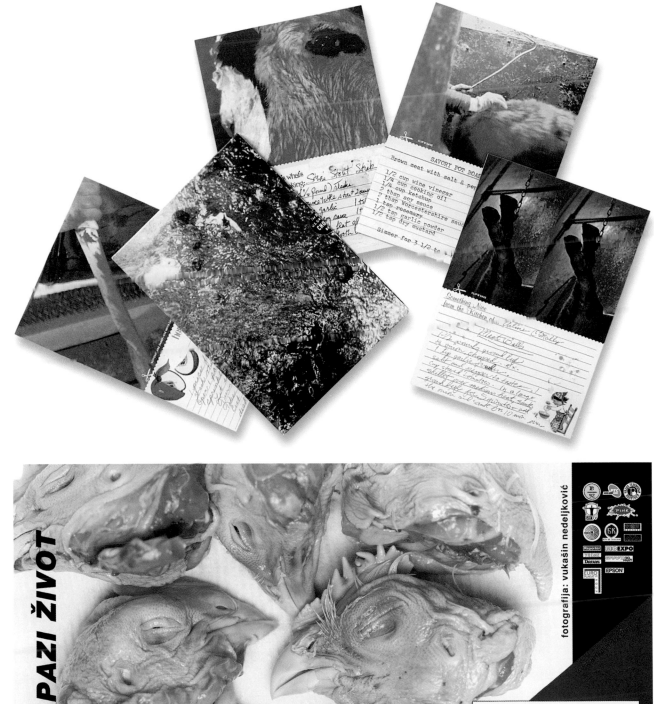

Title: **Life**
Format: **Billboard**
Art Director/Designer:
Stanislav Sharp
Photographer:
Vukašin Nedeljković
Client: **No client**
Country: **Serbia and Montenegro**
Year: **2002**

This billboard campaign promoting a vegetarian lifestyle was designed with a double meaning in mind. The disturbing image of chicken heads shown much larger than life also reminds viewers to "preserve life," theirs, and the lives of other humans.

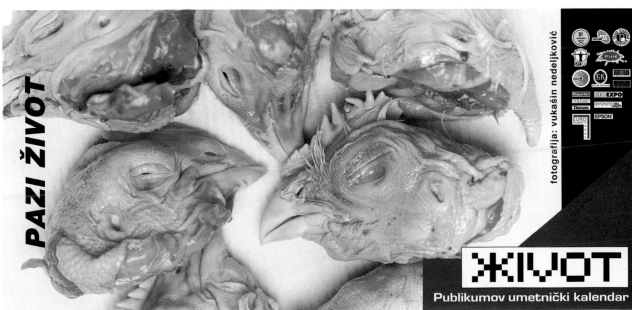

Title: **Death**
Format: **T-shirt**
Art Director/Designer:
Tyler Galloway
Client: **No client**
Country: **USA**
Year: **1998**

The poetic discovery of the word "eat" within the word "death" creates the opportunity to remind consumers that the pleasures of one species require the blood of another.

Who died for your dyed fur?

peta2.com

Fake color doesn't mean fake fur.

peta2.com

Title: **Dyed Fur**
Format: **Print ad**
Art Director/Designer:
Sandra Scher
Client: **PETA**
Country: **USA**
Year: **2004**

The animal activist group PETA, which introduced a series of aggressive anti-fur ads in the 1980s, sponsored this campaign to alert people to the fact that fur now comes in bright colors, because the fur industry has been dying fur in the hopes that young women will mistake it for faux.

Title: Equal Treatment
Format: **Ad campaign**
Art Director/Designer:
Sandra Scher
Client: **PETA**
Country: **USA**
Year: **2003**

This ad campaign highlights the hypocrisy inherent in being an animal lover while eating meat. It raises the question of why people who would go out of their way to keep a pet would turn a blind eye to the suffering of animals on factory farms.

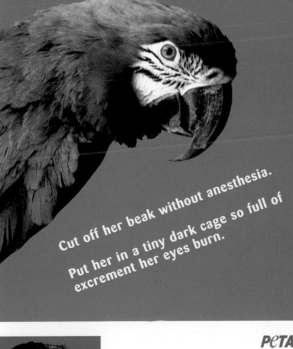

A manifesto

We, the undersigned, are graphic designers, photographers and students who have been brought up in a world in which the techniques and apparatus of advertising have persistently been presented to us as the most lucrative, effective and desirable means of using our talents. We have been bombarded with publications devoted to this belief, applauding the work of those who have flogged their skill and imagination to sell such things as:

cat food, stomach powders, detergent, hair restorer, striped toothpaste, aftershave lotion, beforeshave lotion, slimming diets, fattening diets, deodorants, fizzy water, cigarettes, roll-ons, pull-ons and slip-ons.

By far the greatest time and effort of those working in the advertising industry are wasted on these trivial purposes, which contribute little or nothing to our national prosperity.

In common with an increasing number of the general public, we have reached a saturation point at which the high pitched scream of consumer selling is no more than sheer noise. We think that there are other things more worth using our skill and experience on. There are signs for streets and buildings, books and periodicals, catalogues, instructional manuals, industrial photography, educational aids, films, television features, scientific and industrial publications and all the other media through which we promote our trade, our education, our culture and our greater awareness of the world.

We do not advocate the abolition of high pressure consumer advertising: this is not feasible. Nor do we want to take any of the fun out of life. But we are proposing a reversal of priorities in favour of the more useful and more lasting forms of communication. We hope that our society will tire of gimmick merchants, status salesmen and hidden persuaders, and that the prior call on our skills will be for worthwhile purposes. With this in mind, we propose to share our experience and opinions, and to make them available to colleagues, students and others who may be interested.

Edward Wright
Geoffrey White
William Slack
Caroline Rawlence
Ian McLaren
Sam Lambert
Ivor Kamlish
Gerald Jones
Bernard Higton
Brian Grimbly
John Garner
Ken Garland
Anthony Froshaug
Robin Fior
Germano Facetti
Ivan Dodd
Harriet Crowder
Anthony Clift
Gerry Cinamon
Robert Chapman
Ray Carpenter
Ken Briggs

Published by Ken Garland.
Printed by Goodwin Press Ltd. London N4

Title: **First Things First**
Format: **Leaflet**
Art Director/Designer: **Ken Garland**
Client: **No client**
Country: **UK**
Year: **1964**

This manifesto organized by Ken Garland brought groups of design professionals together to express their concerns about the direction society was going and raised the question of whether designers can act in concert to improve social conditions. It resonated within the design community at the time and the issues it raised are still vital today.

© GARTH WALKER

THE WORLD WE LIVE IN · GREED IS GOOD · PART 1

SPOT THE DIFFERENCE #17

NAME:	**Wiseman Ndlovu***
AGE:	Late 20's
ADDRESS:	Homeless (Berea Area – Durban)
MARITAL STATUS	Unmarried – Children (Whereabouts Unknown)
EDUCATION:	Grade 8 (Not Completed)
OCCUPATION:	Currently Unemployed – Part time Car Guard
INCOME 2001–2002:	Tips (Approx. $360)
PERSONAL WEALTH:	Clothing and Personal Items – Sports Bag – 2 x Blankets
GENERAL HEALTH:	HIV+ – Persistent Cough – Underweight
PERSONAL DETAILS:	Unfailingly Polite, Trustworthy and Friendly Generally Well Groomed Some in the Area like Wiseman around – but many feel the "Homeless" are a nuisance)
LAST MEAL:	Half Loaf White Bread – 4 Slices Polony Small Portion of Steers Fries 250ml Milk – Half Tin Coke (Donated) 2 Cigarettes (Donated)

NAME:	**Gary Winnick***
AGE:	Early 50's
ADDRESS:	Beverly Hills Los Angeles
MARITAL STATUS	Married – Children
EDUCATION:	College Graduate
OCCUPATION:	Chairman Global Crossing (Bankrupt_Under Investigation)
INCOME 1996–2002:	Salary_Stock_Consulting_Aircraft Ownership $750.8m
PERSONAL WEALTH:	Substantial (Though Significantly Reduced)
GENERAL HEALTH:	Good – Overweight
PERSONAL DETAILS:	With the help of his bankers, Gary Winnick treated Global Crossing as his personal cash cow – until the company went bankrupt On a whim over lunch – bought Global Crossing co-chairman a Rolls Royce – and the CEO an Aston Martin
LAST MEAL:	Pan Asian Seared Mahi-Mahi – Small Side Salad Crème Brulée 2 Glasses Napa Valley Chardonay –250ml Mineral Water

* Based on research

* Based on research_Financial Info_FORTUNE June 24 2002

Title: **Shit Piece (Spot the difference)**
Format: **Magazine spread**
Art Director/Designer: **Garth Walker**
Client: *Design Indaba* magazine
Country: **South Africa**
Year: **2002**

This unpublished piece was commissioned by *Design Indaba*. It was created after the Enron and Worldcom scandals and comments on the outrageous corporate business greed in today's society. The piece points out that when humans are examined at a very basic level, it is clear that we are all equal and there is no difference between the rich and the poor.

Title: **Arm &
Hammer Logo**
Format: **Logo**
Art Director/Designer:
Dejan Krsić
Client: **What, how &
for whom/WHW**
Country: **Croatia**
Year: **2003**

For this logo and signage
for the independent
curators interested in
socially conscious
contemporary art, WHW–
what, how and for whom,
the Arm & Hammer logo
has been re-imagined by
replacing the company
name with the famous
Fluxus slogan, "Art is not a
mirror, it is a hammer!"
The Zagreb designers did
not realize at the time that
the owner of the American
baking soda company, Arm
& Hammer, had a cozy
relationtionship with the
Soviet Union.

Title: **Globalization**
Format: **Sticker
and poster**
Art Director/Designers:
**Dejan Krsić,
Dejan Dragosavac Rutta**
Client: **IPEG
(Initiative Against
Economy Globalization)**
Country: **Croatia**
Year: **2000**

This anti-globalization
sticker, which reads
"For Globalization of
Freedom and not Corporate
Power," was created
for anti-globalization
demonstrations held in
Zagreb, Croatia at the time
of an international meeting
of economic superpowers
organized by an ad hoc
coalition of various
non-governmental
organizations.

LOS CAMPESINOS DEL MUNDO
APLASTARAN LA GLOBALIZACION

FARM WORKERS OF THE WORLD, UNITE! SMASH THE WTO! 세계의 노동자는 WTO를 탄압한다.

Title: **Hermano Kyang Hae Lee**
Format: **Poster**
Art Director/Designer: **Favianna Rodriguez**
Client: **No client**
Country: **USA**
Year: **Unknown**

This poster calls on farmers to unite against globalization and WTO's policies that hurt farmers in third-world countries.

Title: **That's Entertainment!**
Format: **Poster**
Art Director/Designer:
Ward Sutton
Client: **No client**
Country: **USA**
Year: **2003**

The collaboration of news and entertainment produces soldiers as beholden to commercial endorsements as any professional athlete,

Title: **Corporate American Flag**
Format: **Magazine cover**
Art Director/Designer:
Shi-Zhe Yung
Client: *Adbusters*
Country: **Canada**
Year: **2003**

The corporate American flag, with logos in place of stars, has been embraced by Americans who want to declare independence from corporate rule. The image has been re-created into an actual flag used in protests and displayed in communities across the United States and around the world.

Title: **Lucky Strike**
Format: **Poster**
Art Director/Designers:
**Agnieszka Dellfina,
Thomas Dellert-Dellacroix**
Client: **No client**
Country: **France**
Year: **1983**

The central image in this collaged poster is a 1965 cover of *LIFE* magazine depicting a blindfolded and gagged Viet Cong man. The crude implementation of commercial products and the words "war is good business" gives it a certain strength that might not have been present with a more professional execution.

Title: **Happy Meal: Gypsies, Tramps and Thieves Mark III**
Format: **Poster**
Art Director/Designer: **Damion Steele**
Client: **No client**
Country: **USA**
Year: **2002**

This homage to Da Vinci's *Last Supper* features the McDonalds characters, Hitler, the Bush Administration, Uncle Sam, and a variety of comic characters in a "happy meal," to demonstrate that "fundamentalist zealots and corporations rule our land."

Title: **McDubya**
Format: **Poster**
Art Director/Designer: **Rebecca Bughouse**
Client: **No client**
Country: **USA**
Year: **2004**

By flipping one of the most recognizable trademarks in the world, this designer relates George "Dubya" Bush's tactics in promoting his wars to McDonald's relentless marketing to sell its burgers. McDonald's tagline "I'm lovin' it" has been changed to "I'm bombin' it," posing the question: Are consumers willing to buy a war if it is marketed as ambitiously as our manufactured goods?

Title: **Weapons of Mass Destruction**
Format: **Postcard**
Art Director/Designer:
Chaz Maviyane-Davies
Client: **No client**
Country: **USA**
Year: **2004**

The designer ponders,
"What are the products
of globalization—the silent
war?" Often the most
pervasive and damaging
can seem to be the most
innocuous. This postcard
is from a series of four
entitled "The Language
of War."

Title: **Coca-Colonization**
Format: **Poster**
Art Director/Designer:
Chaz Maviyane-Davies
Client: **No client**
Country: **USA**
Year: **2000**

This work illuminating
corporate global branding
in third-world countries
was run in *Adbusters*
magazine.

Title: **No to the War**
Format: **Poster and T-shirt**
Art Director/Designer: **Andrés Mario Ramírez Cuevas**
Client: **Multiforo Alicia**
Country: **Mexico**
Year: **2003**

Although this image was created to oppose the war in Iraq, it also refers to a larger war between indigenous cultures and the global reach of American corporations, symbolized by Coca-Cola's branding elements, as they supersede the values and economies of the regions they enter.

Title: **Act Against Globalization**
Format: **Poster**
Art Director/Designer:
Richardt Strydom
Client: **No client**
Country: **South Africa**
Year: **Unknown**

This simple yet powerful image urges viewers to "Employ Molotov" in the fight against globalization. In 1941, the Red Army suffered from "ammo starvation" so petrol bombs were employed to use against tanks. These "bombs," made from fuel and empty glass bottles, were quickly dubbed "Molotov Cocktails." Molotov, during the war years, was Stalin's leading lieutenant, Politburo member, GKO (State Defense Committee) and Sovnarkom vice-chairman.

Title: **United Colors of Netanyahu**
Format: **Poster**
Art Director/Designer: **David Tartakover**
Photographer: **David Krap**
Client: **No client**
Country: **Israel**
Year: **1998**

By playing on racial, ethnic, and religious stereotypes, the fashion company Benetton often used its United Colors campaign to create provocative ads loaded with social commentary. Created during his tenure as Israel's Prime Minister, this poster contrasts the image of Benjamin Netanyahu as a family man with the security requirements that now characterize life in Israel. *(top)*

UNITED COLORS OF NETANYAHU.

Title: **United Colors of Serbia**
Format: **Magazine cover**
Art Director/Designer: **Vladan Srdić**
Client: *Kvadart* **magazine**
Country: **Slovenia**
Year: **1999**

This magazine cover parodies the "United Colors of Benetton" campaign to convey that the actual color of Serbia is black—five lost wars in ten years; enormous inflation; one president in prison, the other killed; poverty; and isolation clearly make the case. *(bottom left)*

Title: **United Colors of Hung(a)ry 2000**
Format: **Poster**
Art Director/Designer: **Péter Pócs**
Client: **No client**
Country: **Hungary**
Year: **2000**

This "Thesis-Synthesis" poster illustrates the transformation of the Hungarian Communist Party symbol into the symbol of its successor, the Hungarian Socialist Party. *(bottom right)*

UNITED COLORS OF SERBIA

UNITED COLORS OF HUNG(A)RY 2000.

TÉÉZI IS - SSZI NNTÉÉZI IS

Title: **War Wear Rifle**
Format: **Poster**
Art Director/Designer:
Tomato Košir
Client: **No client**
Country: **Slovenia**
Year: **2000**

Rifle is a trendy Italian
jeans company that targets
what they call the
"cyberpunk generation."
Created as an anti-war
poster, this simple yet
potent imagery contrasts
the frivolity of our
consumer-driven lifestyle
with the horror of war.

Title: **VW Spoof Ad**
Format: **Poster**
Art Director/Designer:
Matt Erceg
Client: **No client**
Country: **USA**
Year: **2001**

This design spoofs ads
for the cute Volkswagen
everyone loves by remind-
ing the viewer who was
responsible for supporting
the development of the
original "people's car," as
they were known when
first produced in Germany,
by inserting an image of
Hitler in his own
Volkswagen.

Title: **Hummer**
Format: **Magazine spread**
Art Director/Designer:
Matt Campbell
Client: *BIG* **magazine**
Country: **USA**
Year: **2004**

These ads attacking SUV ownership were designed by a group called Greedy Gas Guzzlers for *BIG* magazine. The images that were allowed to run were ultimately reduced to thumbnails because Hummer objected to them and would not advertise in the magazine unless they were removed.

Title: **Pay Us to Kill You**
Format: **Poster**
Art Director/Designer:
G. Dan Covert
Client: **California College of the Arts**
Country: **USA**
Year: **2001**

This artist's grandmother passed away after a long battle with emphysema, which provoked this poster focusing on how profitable the tobacco industry has been while promoting illness and death.

Title: **Los Gatos California: What Right Do They Take Away Next?**
Format: **T-shirt**
Art Director/Designer: **Unknown**
Client: **Unknown**
Country: **USA**
Year: **Unknown**

This reaction to a nonsmoking ban in bars and restaurants in Los Gatos, California, one of the first municipalities that enforced the ban on smoking, included T-shirts that were given to municipal officers as protest gifts to show their displeasure with this policy.

Title: **Don't Smoke**
Format: **Poster**
Art Director/Designers: **Albino Uršić, Boris Kuk**
Client: **No client**
Country: **Croatia**
Year: **1994**
Dušan Petričić

Nazi images, which immediately get viewers' attention and allude to the idea of gas chambers, suggest that cigarette companies do not care if they kill you.

STOP THE ARROGANCE

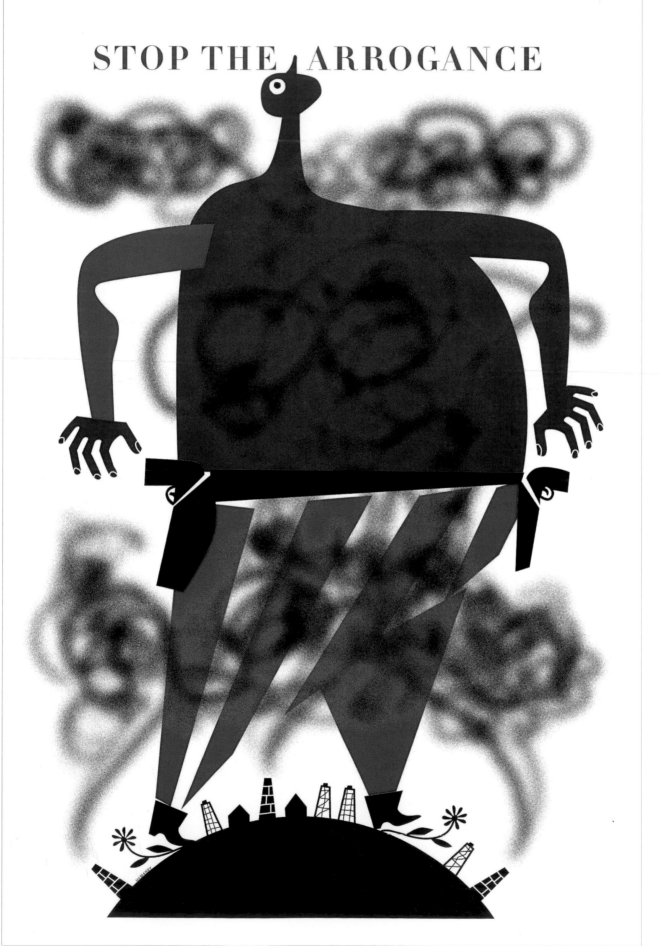

Title: **Stop the Arrogance**
Format: **Poster**
Art Director/Designers:
**Nicholas Blechman,
Michael Mabry**
Client: *NOZONE
IX/EMPIRE*
Country: **USA**
Year: **2003**

This poster, entered in an
exhibition sponsored by the
Hong Kong International
Poster Triennial 2004,
expresses the frustrations
U.S. citizens have with the
Bush Administration's lack
of environmental policies.
The gun-slinging cowboy,
"trashing everything in its
path" while polluting the
air and water, reflects not
only the United States
government's lack of
interest in protecting the
environment, but also the
arrogance and lack of
caring for the general
welfare of the rest of the
Earth.

Title: **Stop the Plant**
Format: **Poster**
Art Director/Designer:
Woody Pirtle/Pentagram
Client: **Scenic Hudson**
Country: **USA**
Year: **2003**

This poster was a part of a grassroots campaign against the construction of a mammoth cement plant that would emit 20 million pounds of pollutants each year on the east bank of the Hudson in upstate New York. Environmental preservation and concerned citizen groups sponsored the campaign.

BRAINWASHING

Title: **Brainwashing**
Format: **Magazine ad**
Art Director/Designer:
Vladan Srdić
Client: *Mlandia* **magazine**
Country: **Slovenia**
Year: **2003**

This image of a dial on a washing machine, labeled with the major television netwoks in America, protests the manipulation of the American mass media, who brainwash the public to support war and aggression.

Title: Your Death—Our Business!
Format: **Poster**
Art Director/Designers:
**Agnieszka Dellfina,
Thomas Dellert-Dellacroix**
Client: **No client**
Country: **France**
Year: **2002**

War is good business, especially for news organizations. Sensationalistic news always attracts viewers and, thus, advertising dollars.

Title: **Reality TV**
Format: **Poster**
Art Director/Designer:
Peter Kuper
Client:
AnotherPosterforPeace.org
Country: **USA**
Year: **2002**

This ghostly downloadable image playing off the abundance of reality shows dominating the networks was produced for antiwar marches in NYC before the Iraq War began.

Title: **Breaking News**
Format: **Postcard**
Art Director/Designer:
Ward Sutton
Client: **No client**
Country: **USA**
Year: **2003**

Embedded American journalists were seduced and manipulated into becoming propagandists during the Iraq War, dutifully reporting the toppling of the Saddam Hussein statue in the news media. This postcard served as an invitation/ announcement for an event the artist sponsored on the failing of the media.

Title: **Independence**
Format: **Poster**
Art Director/Designer:
Sonja Smith
Client: **No client**
Country: **USA**
Year: **2003**

This personal expression of dissent was created by the artist for posting in the street on 4th of July (Independence Day), 2003, in opposition to corporate control of the media.

Title: **Media Democracy Day**
Format: **Poster and logo**
Art Director/Designer:
Valerie Thai
Client: **Campaign for Press and Broadcast Freedom**
Country: **Canada**
Year: **2002–2003**

The image of a clenched fist as a speech balloon was created for Canada's Media Democracy Day created to protest the dominant mass media system and promote independent media and citizens fighting for their right to news and information, and their basic right to communicate their opinions.

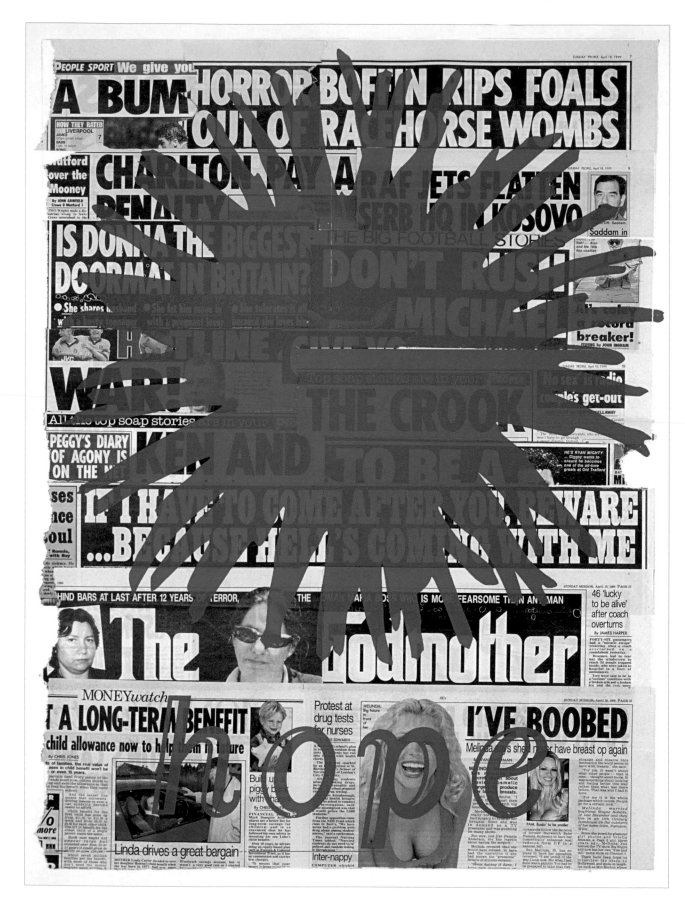

Title: **Hope**
Format: **Poster**
Art Director/Designer:
Charlie Ross
Client: **No client**
Country: **USA**
Year: **1999**

This poster encourages the public to transcend the overwhelming presence of tabloid media and its obsession with violence and scandal. The artist comments, "To believe you can move beyond your mistakes, to me, defines hope."

Title: As Seen on TV
Format: Poster
Art Director/Designer:
Jeff Louviere
Client: The American™
Dream
Country: USA
Year: 2000

The image is provocative, but the statistic noting that, by the age of 18, American children will have witnessed 16,000 murders on television is even more so.

Title: **Dźihad**
Format: **Poster**
Art Director/Designer:
Ewa Wlostowska
Client: **No client**
Country: **Poland**
Year: **2002**

Magritte's everyday man here serves to represent the idea of an ordinary European being connected to Jihad. The figure is a secret fighter ready to assume the green color of Jihad and start fighting for the cause at a moment's notice.

Title: **Impuls**
Format: **Poster**
Art Director/Designer:
Ewa Wlostowska
Client: **No client**
Country: **Poland**
Year: **2002**

This poster utilizes the simplicity of a symbol to suggest a broader message about the transmission of ideas and information. This artist's suggestion is that to be recognized one must make waves or send impulses throughout the world. The symbol used here is one that has come to represent Islam, the crescent and the star.

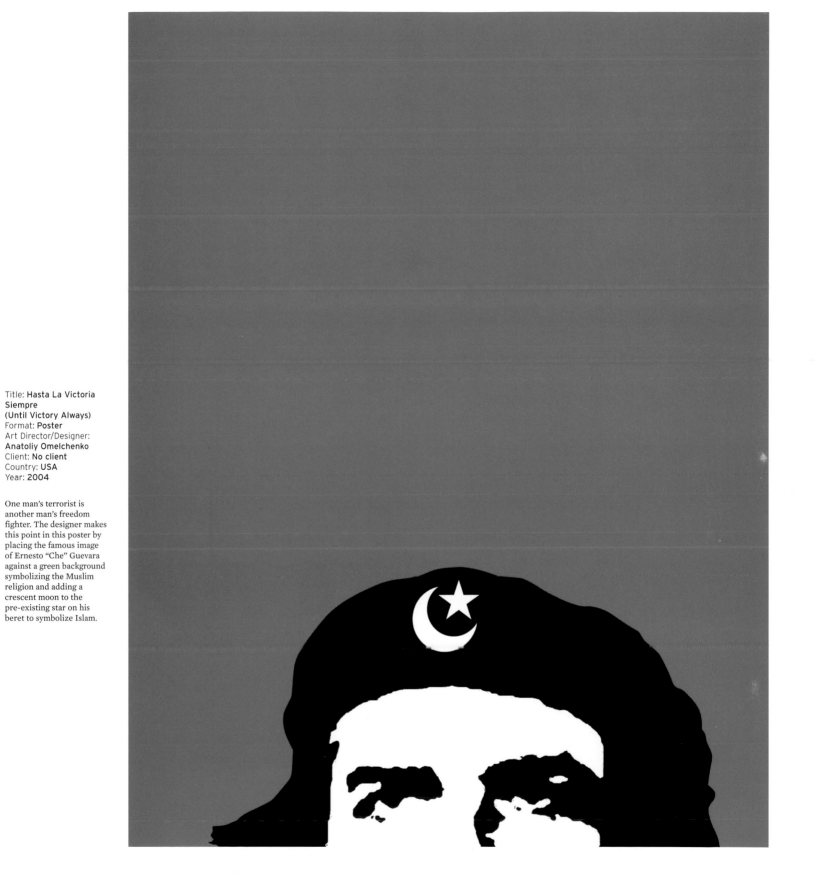

Title: **Hasta La Victoria
Siempre**
(Until Victory Always)
Format: **Poster**
Art Director/Designer:
Anatoliy Omelchenko
Client: **No client**
Country: **USA**
Year: **2004**

One man's terrorist is
another man's freedom
fighter. The designer makes
this point in this poster by
placing the famous image
of Ernesto "Che" Guevara
against a green background
symbolizing the Muslim
religion and adding a
crescent moon to the
pre-existing star on his
beret to symbolize Islam.

Title: **Medals
of Dishonour**
Format: **Postcard**
Art Director/Designer:
Chaz Maviyane-Davies
Client: **No client**
Country: **USA**
Year: **2002**

This piece was created in
response to a statement
made by defense forces
commander General Vitalis
Zvinavashe, the day that
President Robert Mugabe
kicked off his campaign, in
which he noted that he and
the security organizations
would not support anyone
with a "different agenda
that threatens the
very existence of our
sovereignty, our country,
and our people."

Title: **DRC/Impunity/
Fear Is the Best Weapon**
Format: **Postcards**
Art Director/Designer:
Chaz Maviyane-Davies
Client: **No client**
Country: **USA**
Year: **2002**

This postcard telling viewers "Do not be intimidated. Use your vote and be counted. Our fear is their best weapon." is a response to the redeployment of the 5th Brigade into Matebeleland, which added a psychological twist to the continued intimidation campaign in Zimbabwe.

The designer comments, "Robert Mugabe sent our troops to die in a war in the Democratic Republic of Congo. It had nothing to do with the interest of the citizens of Zimbabwe but with his personal greed." *(opposite bottom left)*

"T-shirts are a life-and-death matter in Zimbabwe. Wear an opposition T-shirt and you become a walking target. The ruling party's (ZANU) T-shirt, on the other hand, allows the wearer immunity from the authorities." This design converts the A to the anarchist symbol to reflect the current reality. *(opposite bottom right)*

Title: *Republicanism*
Format: **Book cover**
Art Director/Designer:
Bijan Sayfouri
Client: **Tarh-e Now
Publishers**
Country: **Iran**
Year: **Unknown**

This cover for
*Republicanism:
Demystification of Power*
depicts King Tahmash,
leader of the historic
Iranian dictatorship, being
obscured by democracy,
represented by a voting
box, as a means of
contrasting these two
types of societies.

Title: The Grim Reaper
Format: Newspaper cartoon
Illustrator: Ali Ferzat
Client: *Al Domari* newspaper
Country: Syria
Year: Mid-'90s

Because of this and similar cartoons published in Ferzat's newspaper *Al Domari*, the only privately owned newspaper in Syria, the Syrian government newspaper published editorials against Ferzat two days in a row, proclaiming it was shameful to make fun of the Iraqi regime while it boldly stood up against superpower invaders. In addition, hundreds of protesters picketed *Al Domari's* offices. *(top)*

Title: *Dictators in the Mirror of Medicine*
Format: Book cover
Art Director/Designer: Bijan Sayfouri
Client: Agah Publishing House
Country: Iran
Year: Unknown

This cover for the book *Dictators in the Mirror of Medicine: Napoleon, Hitler and Stalin* represents Hitler as a psychopath, the universal symbol of cruel dictatorship across borders. *(bottom left)*

Title: Right to Information
Format: Poster
Art Director/Designer: Sanjeev Bothra
Client: MKSS—Majdur, Kisan, Shakti, Sangathan
Country: India
Year: 2001

The triangular intersection of politician, police, and bureaucrat illustrates the endemic corruption in India. This poster was commissioned by an Indian nongovernmental agency sponsoring a workshop called, "The Right to Information." The text on the poster notes that the state has been ruled under the shadow of scams and that too much theft has taken place. It asks "Someone speak up, at least open your mouth." *(bottom right)*

Title: **Banners for March**
Format: **Banners**
Art Director/Designer:
Ken Garland
Client: **CND**
Country: **UK**
Year: **1963**

Ken Garland worked with Peggy Duff to pull together this groundbreaking protest in which they provided various branches of the campaign for Nuclear Disarmament with stencils, black fabric, and specifications on banner content and height. Each branch was asked to stencil their name on one side of the banner and a slogan on the reverse, which involved the participants in the event on a more immediate level. The participants then surrounded Windsor Castle in its entirety—a feat no longer possible in today's society.

Title: **Puzzle Pieces**
Format: **Illustration, sign**
Art Director/Designer:
Rebecca Migdal
Client: **No client**
Country: **USA**
Year: **2003**

The puzzle showing how various events link up to complete a large historical picture was designed at a World War III Arts in Action workshop. The pieces were later used as a group of signs during a massive 2004 peace rally in New York City.

Title: **Free Trade Area of the Americas**
Format: **Banner**
Art Director/Designer:
Behive Design Collective
Client: **anti-copyright non-profit**
Country: **USA**
Year: **Unknown**

The Free Trade Area of the Americas (FTAA), which has been negotiated in private since 1994, aims to eliminate the remaining "barriers" to the free flow of money, goods, and services across borders in the Western Hemisphere, excluding Cuba, in an attempt to create one huge, integrated web of "open markets." This graphic representation of it illustrates the consequences of this network, and exposes its threat to all forms of life throughout the Americas and is a tool for educating people about the overwhelming effects of a monoculture. *(top)*

Title: **Poder**
Format: **Installation**
Art Director/Designers:
Grupo Calljero Periferia/ Benites, Corda, Doberti, Kuperman, and Zech
Client: **People of Buenos Aires City**
Country: **Argentina**
Year: **2002**

On December 20, 2001, Argentinians went to the streets demanding that banks give back their savings, which had been confiscated to pay Argentina's debt. This ultimately caused the collapse of the government and resulted in twenty-nine deaths. One year later, the urban art group Periferia conjugated the verb "poder" (which means "power" and "can") on a fence erected one year previous to protect the "government's house," the embodiment of corrupt power. *(bottom left)*

Title: **Siamo Uomini o Cavalieri?**
Format: **Poster**
Art Director/Designer:
Andrea Rauch
Client: **CGIL (Italian Syndicate)**
Country: **Italy**
Year: **2002**

Totó, Italy's beloved actor is used here to pose his well-remembered question, "Are we men or foremen?" in reference to allegedly corrupt Italian Prime Minister Berlusconi, who owns and controls most of the media in Italy. In Italian, "foreman" carries negative connotations of one who torments other men. *(bottom right)*

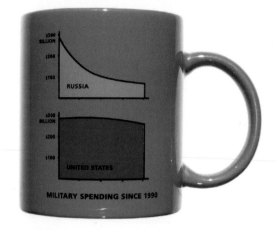

Title: **Move Our Money**
Format: **Various**
Art Director/Designers:
**Stefan Sagmeister,
Hjalti Karlsson**
Client: **Business Leaders
for Sensible Priorities**
Country: **USA**
Year: **1999**

The familiar Crayola colors and simple designs in this series of works make the huge, complex Pentagon budget figures comprehensible and simple. Some of the charts, designed as enormous inflatable sculptures, formed part of a traveling road show featuring the Move Our Money mobile. These displays provided a little (but hopefully hard-hitting) information on a large scale. Other items such as T-shirts, statistic cards, and pens were given away to spectators during the traveling show. Ben Cohen, of Ben & Jerry's ice cream, formed Business Leaders for Sensible Priorities, an initiative to move 15 percent of the Pentagon budget to education and health care.

Title: **True Majority**
Format: **Various**
Art Director/Designers:
Stefan Sagmeister,
Matthias Ernstberger
Client: **True Majority**
Country: **USA**
Year: **2002**

This logo was designed for a grassroots education and advocacy group led by Ben Cohen (cofounder of Ben & Jerry's) and comprised of 200 business leaders, CEOs, and military advisers. The group's goals are to pressure the government to adopt long-term policies designed to prevent another 9/11 by dealing with world hunger, reducing dependence on oil, and paying our UN dues. *(top left)*

These pink piggy cars compare and contrast the Pentagon budget (the first pink car in line) to the spending on education (the second pink car) and foreign aid (the third). *(top right)*

These cars, which focus on saving energy, conserving the environment, and reducing our oil dependence, are being driven throughout the United States. The designer notes, "As a base, the hybrid Toyota Prius was used. If all cars on the road in the United States would achieve the same gas mileage as the Prius, no Middle East oil would have to be imported." The goal was to get the cars featured on local TV news channels, thereby forcing newscasters to explain what the campaign was about. *(bottom)*

Title: **Swimming Against the Tide**
Format: **Poster**
Art Director/Designer: **John Yates**
Client: **Stealworks**
Country: **USA**
Year: **Unknown**

In the tradition of John Heartfield's powerful photomontaged *AIZ* magazine covers, this poster juxtaposes a peaceful street scene from the "Golden Fifties" with a diametrically opposed one of urban warfare.

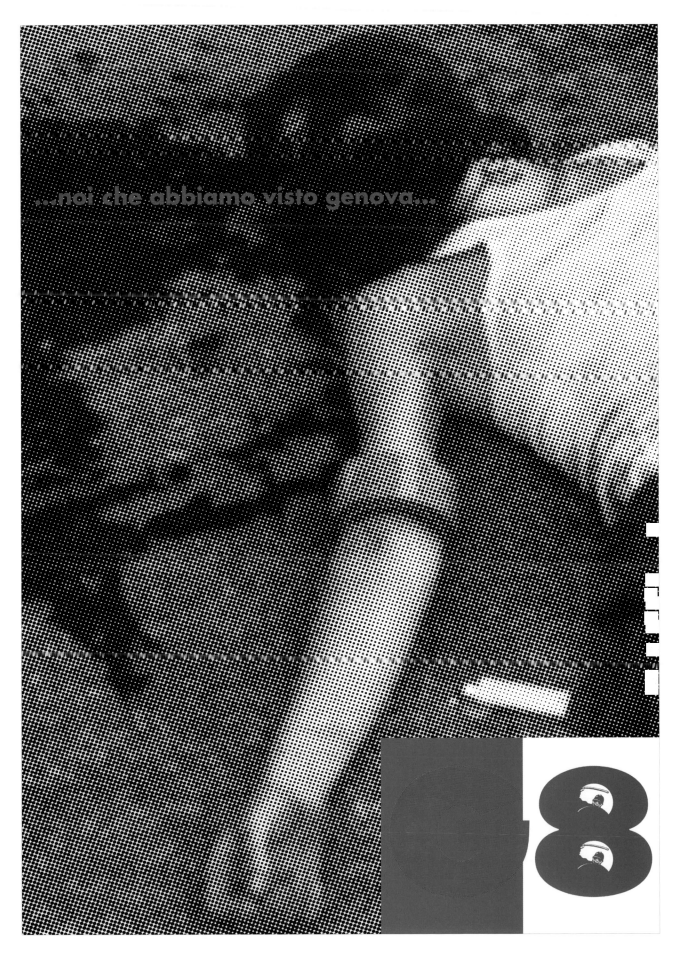

...noi che abbiamo visto genova...

Title: **G8**
Format: **Poster**
Art Director/Designer:
Andrea Rauch
Client: **ARCI**
Country: **Italy**
Year: **2001**

Prior to the 2001 G8
Summit in which the
leaders of Canada, France,
Germany, Italy, Japan,
Russia, the United
Kingdom, and the United
States met in Genova, Italy,
Silvio Berlusconi govern-
ment claimed it would
guarantee the right to
peaceful protest.
However, this claim was
swept aside during the
resulting widespread
demonstrations. Clashes
between the police and
protestors resulted in 482
injuries and 280 arrests.
Perhaps the most dramatic
moment occurred when
Italian police shot dead
activist Carlo Giuliani. The
caption of this poster reads,
"We have seen Genova."
The counter spaces of the
"8" have been replaced by
stylized illustrations of
police with clubs raised.

Title: **Die Toten**
Format: **Poster series**
Art Director/Designer:
Fons Hickmann
Client: **No client**
Country: **Germany**
Year: **Unknown**

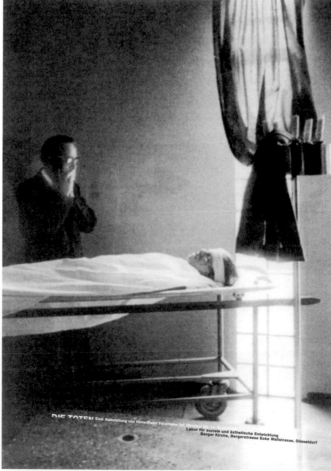

These posters announce an exhibit by Hans-Peter Feldman based on a period of RAF (Red Army Faction) left-wing terrorism in West Germany from 1968 to 1985. One poster uses a photograph of RAF member Elisabeth von Dyck moments before the German Secret Service killed her in their attempt to arrest her. The other is a photograph of RAF member Petra Schelm's dead body attended by his father. Each poster announces the times and dates of the exhibit, along with the exhibit title "Die Toten," which means "The Dead."

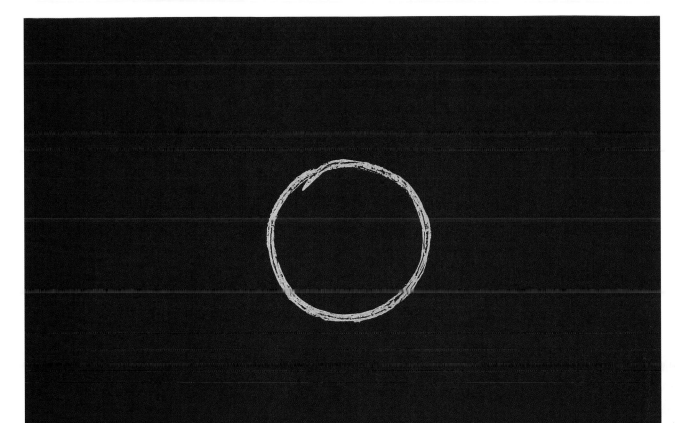

Wer nicht wählt, wählt rechtsextrem, wer rechtsextrem wählt, wählt besser nicht.

Title: **links/rechts**
Format: **Poster**
Art Director/Designers:
Lars Harmsen,
Ulrich Weiß, Lutz Wahler,
Michael Lutz
Client: **Gruppe 10**
Country: **Germany**
Year: **1994**

Every other month Gruppe 10 sends a magazine, a poster collection, a slide-show etc. to its subscribers. This image is part of a collection of posters that was sent out a few weeks before the chancellor election in Germany. The title plays on the words "left" and "right," to illustrate that people don't know what they are voting for.

THE SILENT MAJORITY

Title: **The Silent Majority**
Format: **Poster**
Art Director/Designer:
Primo Angeli
Photographer: **Lars Speyer**
Client: **No client**
Country: **Italy**
Year: **1969**

The headline of this poster refers to comments made by President Nixon in which he demeaned protesters by deeming those who supported the war as "the silent majority." This designer proposes that the true silent majority is composed of soldiers buried in the Colma military cemetery in California under tombstones bearing numbers rather than names.

Title: **Resist Empire**
Format: **Buttons**
Art Director/Designer:
Kyle Goen
Client: **No client**
Country: **USA**
Year: **2004**

This series of buttons is intended to encourage people to read the works by the authors featured. Unfortunately, identifying stickers are placed inside the buttons, which only helps the owner of the button. It's the long running Blackgama mink ad problem—it only works if the photograph is of someone instantly recognizable, a real legend.

(top left to right) Amy Goodman, Arundhati Roy, Tariq Ali (bottom left to right) Angela Y. Davis, Noam Chomsky, Edward Said

Title: **React Manual**
Format: **Booklet**
Art Director/Designers:
Tom Sieu, John Givens
Client: **Amnesty**
International
Country: **USA**
Year: **2003**

The React Manual for
Amnesty was an activism
tool kit designed to urge
sixteen- to twenty-five-
year-olds to stand up
against oppression and
repressive government. The
kit included information on
how individuals could get
involved, as well as a CD
containing messaging
templates, such as letters to
congressmen and women,
and banners that people
could customize and use.

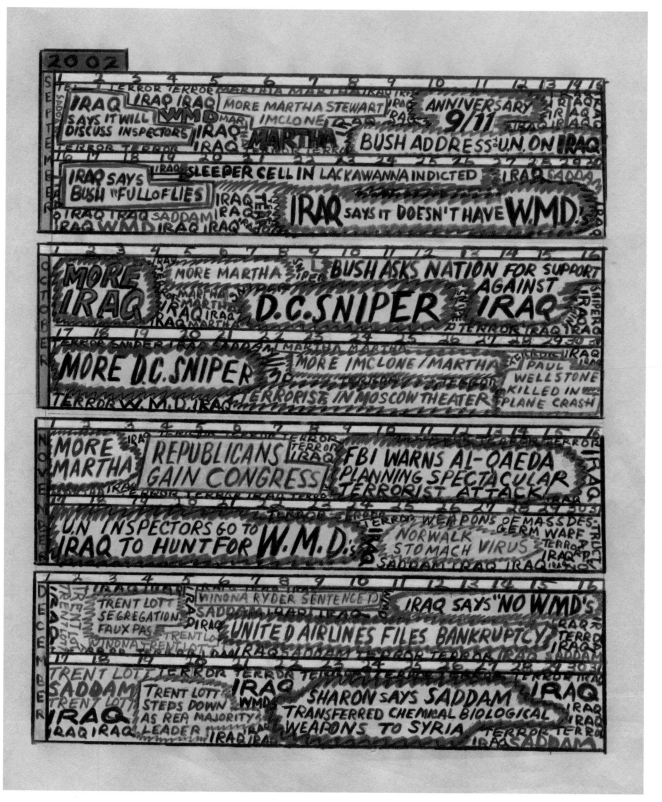

Title: **All the News That Fits**
Format: **Visual essay**
Art Director/Designer:
Paula Scher
Client: *Print* magazine
Country: **USA**
Year: **2001-2003**

This visual essay, which appeared in *Print* magazine, records in a personal and powerful way, the texture of the news before and after 9/11. The author, Paula Scher, observes "The news abruptly switched from a background of sex to a background of terror, without missing a beat." The image shown is only a small portion of the work.

Title: Illustrated Letters
Format: **Electronic images**
Art Director/Designer:
Nikola Djurek
Client: **Rick Valicenti/Thirst**
Country: **Croatia**
Year: **2003–2004**

The artist used photographs that he took of the television news over a two year time period to create an interpretative alphabet that shows the current world we live in from his perspective. The images are posted and sold through the website: play-rickvalicenti.com.

Title: **Free Burma**
Format: **Poster/Flyer**
Art Director/Designer:
James Song
Client: **No client**
Country: **USA**
Year: **2004**

The image of a machine gun is suggestively created by the typography in this poster for a rally sponsored by the Free Burma Student Movement in Washington, D.C. The current leader of Burma came into power through a military coup that provoked student opposition.

Title: **Left Right Boom**
Format: **Poster**
Art Director/Designer:
Yarom Vardimon
Client: **Museum of the Seam, Jerusalem**
Country: **Israel**
Year: **2002**

The typographic rhythms of this poster call for tolerance and reflect the militaristic state of affairs in Israel. This piece was displayed outside the German Reichstag as part of the Coexistence Internal traveling exhibition in 2003.

Title: Postcards:
Political Types
Format: **Postcards**
Art Director/Designers:
**Sonia Freeman,
Gabriel Freeman**
Client: **LSDspace**
Country: **Spain**
Year: **Unknown**

This variation of Arial appropriates a loaded symbol to evoke power and fear. Along with an expletive, these cards read, "No one must be authorized in spoiling what nature has created for the sake of racial evolution. Your highest purpose in life should be to better maintain this evolution toward a better, stronger, and beautiful humanity."

Title: **Postcards:
Political Types**
Format: **Postcards**
Art Director/Designers:
**Sonia Freeman,
Gabriel Freeman**
Client: **LSDspace**
Country: **Spain**
Year: **Unknown**

Futura suggests concepts of legibility and coherence, concepts associated with order and rationality. This font becomes illegible and therefore irrational when the letters "s," "a," and "n" are crossed out. These read, "Fraternity, liberty, equality, inhumanity" and "Without future...to be poor is to be hungry, to lack shelter and clothing is to be illiterate and not receive information."

Hijoputa!

Arial Symbol www.lsdspace.com

Arial Symbol www.lsdspace.com Robin Nicholas and Patricia Saunders

Nadie debe ser autorizado en malograr lo que la naturaleza creó en aras de la evolución racial. Tu más elevado propósito en la vida ha de ser el de mantener dicha evolución hacia una humanidad mejor, más fuerte y bella. La pureza de la más elevada de las razas es el requisito esencial para cualquier evolución superior. (III. TEN FE EN TU RAZA)

Raza

Arial Symbol www.lsdspace.com

xin futuro

no es sólo pobreza económica (menos de un dólar al día). "Ser pobre es tener hambre, carecer de cobijo y ropa, estar enfermo y no ser atendido, ser iletrado y no recibir formación; supone vulnerabilidad ante los adversidades y a menudo padecer mal trato y exclusión de las instituciones".

sin futuro (después de paul renner)   www.lsdspace.com

**ABCDEFGHIJKLM
NÑOPQRSTUVW
XYZ. FUTUR**
paul renner   www.lsdspace.com

**frater idad
libert d
igu ld d
i hum idad**

derecho humano = in futur   www.lsdspace.com

POP QUIZ

BY OPEN, N.Y. FOR MOVEON.ORG

Q: WHO SAID "I WILL LEAVE NO CHILD BEHIND" AND THEN CUT $6 BILLION OF EDUCATION FUNDING?

SOURCE: The New York Times

A: GEORGE W. BUSH.

Q: WHO PROMISED $400 BILLION FOR MEDICARE AND THEN BUDGETED ONLY $40 BILLION?

SOURCES: speech 1/29/03 vs. Federal Budget 2004

A: GEORGE W. BUSH.

Q: WHO SUPPORTED A PAY CUT FOR U.S. TROOPS IN THE MIDDLE EAST?

SOURCE: San Francisco Chronicle

A: GEORGE W. BUSH.

Q: WHO WAS THE FIRST U.S. PRESIDENT TO ABANDON AN INTERNATIONAL NUCLEAR ARMS TREATY?

SOURCE: CNN

A: GEORGE W. BUSH.

Q: WHAT'S WRONG WITH THIS PICTURE?

A:

Title: Pop Quiz
Format: Television ad
Art Director/Designers:
Scott Stowell,
Cara Brower,
Susan Barber,
Kate Kittredge
Client: MoveOn.org
Country: USA
Year: 2003

This television spot was created for a contest called "Bush in 30 Seconds" run by the activist organization MoveOn.org. The main goal of the piece was to reach out to Bush supporters with hard facts about the Bush Administration in the hopes of prompting some of them to think twice about who they would vote for in the next election.

Title: **Nobody**
Format: **Yard sign**
Art Director/Designer:
Tyler Galloway
Client: **No client**
Country: **USA**
Year: **2000**

This yard sign proposes that every person contributes in some way to the enrichment of the community. The designer muses, "Imagine participating in free, networked associations of neighbors, neighborhoods, and cities. No hierarchy. No politicians. No hidden agendas. Just direct input. Direct decisions. Direct democracy."

Title: **No More Bu__Sh__!
/Fermez La Bush!**
Format: **Bumper sticker**
Art Director/Designer:
Erena Rae
Client: **No client**
Country: **USA**
Year: **1991/2003**

These bumper stickers use two variations on presidents' names: one, in reference to George H. Bush, is scatological; the other is a response to the boycotting of French wine during George W. Bush's administration. In this instance, "Fermez la Bush" (Close your "mouth") can be read as a message to the French or the American public.

Title: **Bush**
Format: **Poster**
Art Director/Designer:
Andrew Lewis
Client: **No client**
Country: **USA**
Year: **2002**

The United States sinks into darkness as a result of the Bush Presidency.

LIGHT UP THE SKY

The Republicans have every right to meet and choose their candidate in our city without abuse. At the same time, their convention creates an opportunity for all of us to express our disagreement with the culture of militarization and violence that our current leaders represent. It is time to change the meanspirited and abrasive tone of our civic discourse. We need an alternative to the harsh and degrading words and images that have filled our consciousness since the war began.

AN ALTERNATIVE RESPONSE THAT REQUIRES NO PERMIT

On August 30, from dusk to dawn, all citizens who wish to end the Bush presidency can use light as our metaphor. We can gather informally all over the city with candles, flashlights and plastic wands to silently express our sorrow over all the innocent deaths the war has caused. We can gather in groups or march in peaceful confrontation without violence. Violence will only convince the undecided electorate to vote for Bush. Not a word needs to be spoken. The entire world will understand our message. Those of us who live here in rooms with windows on the street can keep our lights on through the night. Imagine, it's 2 or 3 in the morning and our city is ablaze with a silent and overwhelming rebuke... *Light transforms darkness.*

FOR UPDATES, LISTEN TO AIR AMERICA WLIB 1190 AM

www.lightupthesky.org

Title: **Light Up the Sky**
Format: **Poster**
Art Director/Designer:
Milton Glaser
Client: **No client**
Country: **USA**
Year: **2004**

When New York City restricted protesters during the Republican Convention, lighting the city with any means possible became a more viable way of speaking out. "I was thinking about how dreadful the city was going to be during the convention, the rage, the acrimony, the police ... What was needed was a solution that would not create civic disorder." Many protestors participated although media coverage was minimal. It simply didn't have the entertainment value of protestors and police encountering one another.

Title: *The Nation*
Initiative Buttons
Format: **Buttons**
Art Director/Designer:
Milton Glaser
Client: *The Nation*
Country: **USA**
Year: **2003–2004**

The "Dubya" series of buttons was quite popular. John Kerry picked up the theme for a while and used it in his speeches during the campaign.

Title: **Show Your Blue**
Format: **Advertisement**
Art Director/Designer:
Milton Glaser
Client: *The Nation*
Country: **USA**
Year: **2004**

After the 2004 U.S. presidential election, many hoped that a spirit of cooperation might arise. However, the "red" and "blue" states became more polarized than ever. These buttons are a call to action for all those opposed to the spirit and stance of the Bush Administration.

Title: **The Moron Terror**
Format: **Poster**
Art Director/Designer:
Adrienne Burk
Client: **No client**
Country: **USA**
Year: **2004**

In this poster, "The War on Terror," a phrase used incessantly by the Bush Administration, is transformed and coupled with the infamous image of President Bush in his flight suit announcing that the war in Iraq was over. The poster was used at anti-Iraq War protests.

Title: **Richie Bush**
Format: **Comic book**
Art Director/Designer:
Peter Kuper
Client: **No client**
Country: **USA**
Year: **2003**

This comic book, based on an earlier comic character Richie Rich, was used at 2004 presidential election events. The author notes, "The surreal level of lies, hubris, and verbal pretzels we've been asked to swallow by the Bush Administration made the comic book an appropriate vehicle for characterizing them." Inside is a comic homage to Snoopy, Charlie Brown, and Woodstock. Because of this, the issue was seized in 2004 by U.S. Customs because it constituted "clearly piratical copies". After complains and discussions about the First Amendment of free speech, the US Customs changed their decision. *(top left and right)*

Title: **Bushit**
Format: **Die-cut cardboard**
Art Director/Designer:
Mirko Ilić
Copywriter: **Daniel Young**
Client: **Daniel Young**
Country: **USA**
Year: **2004**

Created for shock value, die-cut cardboard was used to create a disconcerting 3-D effect. The pieces were distributed widely on the streets and sidewalks of New York City by the designer and creative director, their collegues, and friends before the 2004 Republican National Convention. *(bottom left)*

Title: **Dum Gum**
Format: **Chewing gum packaging**
Art Director/Designer:
Haley Johnson
Client: **Blue Q**
Country: **USA**
Year: **2004**

The artist speculates who is really dumb: President Bush or the gullible public who buy his lies?
(bottom right)

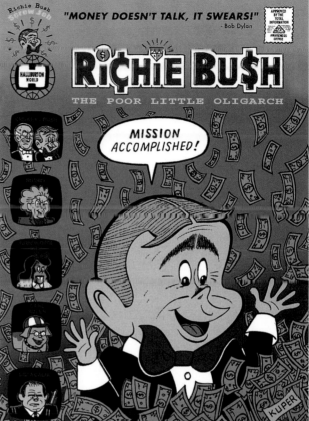

Title: **Republican Rage**
Format: **Poster**
Art Director/Designer:
Ward Sutton
Client: **No client**
Country: **USA**
Year: **2001**

Elephants never forget and neither do Republicans, according to the results of the 2000 election. The artist believes right-wing anger and a mob-rules mentality forced Democratic presidential candidate, Al Gore, into the position of loser. *(top)*

Title: **The Worst Political Ads in America Event**
Format: **Logo**
Art Director/Designers:
**Bill Thorburn,
Travis Olson**
Client: **Growth & Justice**
Country: **USA**
Year: **2004**

Growth & Justice, a nonpartisan public policy institute, stands for civil dialogue. This logo designed for their "The Worst Political Ads in America" fund-raiser plays off the egocentric showoff as well as political parties and their advertising agencies. *(bottom left)*

Title: **Ceci n'est pas une comic**
Format: **Magazine comic**
Art Director/Designer:
Nicholas Blechman
Ilustration: **Peter Kuper**
Client: *NOZONE*
Country: **USA**
Year: **2003**

The comic created for the Empire issue of *NOZONE* magazine plays with the notion of reality compared to what the Bush Administration espouses. The comic borrows images from Magritte's *Ceci n'est pas une pipe* painting, a surreal icon. *(bottom right)*

Title: **We Need
More Party Animals**
Format: **Poster**
Art Director/Designer:
Thomas Porostocky
Client: *Repeat/Defeat*
Newspaper
Country: **USA**
Year: **2004**

This poster was designed as a playful protest against the limited choices imposed by the two-party political system in America.

THE D OF DIS

BY TONY KUSHNER

At the beginning of Stendhal's *The Charterhouse of Parma*, the French army arrives in Milan, whose citizens, under the despotic rule of the Holy Roman Empire, "were still subject to certain minor monarchical restrictions which that continued to vex them. For instance," Stendhal writes:

"the Archduke, who resided in Milan and governed in the name of his cousin the [Holy Roman] Emperor, had conceived the lucrative notion of speculating in wheat.

Consequently, no peasant could sell his crop until His Highness's granaries were full.

In May 1796, three days after the entry of the French, a young miniaturist named Gros, slightly mad and subsequently famous, arrived with the army and overheard talk in the great Caffè dei Servi (fashionable at the time) of the exploits of the Archduke, who happened to be extremely fat. Snatching up the list of ices stamped on a sheet of coarse yellow paper, he drew on the back a French

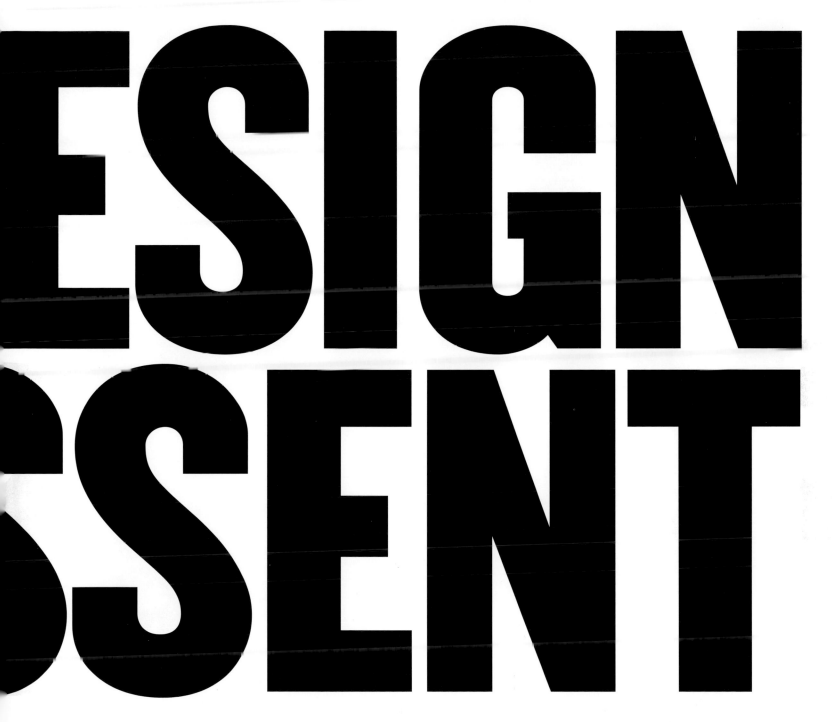

ESIGN
SSENT

soldier thrusting his bayonet into the obese Archduke's belly: instead of blood out poured an incredible quantity of grain. The idea of caricature or cartoon was unknown in this nation of wary despotism. The sketch Gros had left on the table of the Caffè dei Servi seemed a miracle from Heaven; it was printed overnight, and twenty thousand copies were sold the next day.

This image shares with other successful instances of graphic dissent at least three characteristics: It is shocking, it is clever—even funny in a grim sort of way—and its meaning is instantly intelligible. And perhaps it shares one other characteristic: It is, or at least it seems to be, samizdat, dangerous, forbidden. Resistance is sending up a signal flare in the darkness. A scrap of torn menu has been left on a café table, left behind for others to find, others who know what the artist knows—that a violent, unjust, criminal order is overdue for abolishment. Some galling truth that has yet to be organized, formulated, that can't yet be spoken out loud, that can be only grumbled and whispered, some truth that lies imprisoned beneath the surface of public discourse is suddenly, finally liberated, shouted at great volume, a cry of rebellion carrying everywhere at once, a cry all the more powerful for being entirely silent, expressed by a cartoon, entirely visual, needing no words, as if to say, by saying nothing at all: "We all know this truth, all of us have always known what's represented here, that's why it's so recognizable. And it's time to declare the secret openly in public places; it's time to act." As Freud warns us, when the repressed returns, it does so with immense force.

Stendhal chooses Antoine-Jean Gros's little act of graphic design/terrorism to emblematize a turning point of political consciousness, the awakening of an oppressed people to an awareness that "whatever it had hitherto respected was sovereignly absurd and on occasion odious." It had waited in everyone's mind, this public execution of the tyrant, this goring of a greedy aristocrat; it needed only Gros's impulsive, casual, almost-accidental gesture of public articulation, and the collective mind and spirit of the people leapt forward in a lightning rush to greet it, to embrace it, and to act on the Promethean freedom fire it delivered to them. Stendhal is describing one of those images everyone has encountered at least once in his or her life—an image on a poster, brand-new yet long-expected, possessing the power of the Uncanny, as if a complete stranger on the street had stepped up to you and spoken clearly something deeply familiar but also deeply private, something you believed only you or very few others like you believed. Miraculous indeed. The political is the arena of the miraculous, where the collective and the communal, so routinely repressed, so viciously suppressed, stages its returns, where eternal truths and immortal edifices can dissolve in an eye blink, in historical time, where change rather than stasis is the only constant. Marianne Moore describes the miracle of the political perfectly: "That which it is impossible to force, it is impossible to hinder."

It is even more of a miracle that the act of forcing the impossible is, in the history of political revolution, often catalyzed by something as flimsy as a poster plastered on a wall—the perfect poster on the perfect wall at the perfect moment. What's miraculous is not that great graphic design, employing shock, wit, and clarity borne of urgency, can move people to action, to acts of courage and sacrifice, overcoming habit and fear. Art can do that; art is always having those sorts of effects. Art can't change anything except people—but art changes people, and people can make everything change.

What's truly miraculous is that, as hard as it is to make the perfect poster—and it must be

immensely hard—someone nearly always seems to be on hand to do the job when the time demands it. Consider the miracle of John Heartfield, Käthe Kollwitz, Aleksander Rodchenko, Casimir Malevich, Vladimir Tatlin, the designers of ACT UP's SILENCE=DEATH, and the artists who edited and are represented in this volume. The time arrives for a silent truth to become a public truth, a collective truth; the pressure of great human need bids the time arrive. Human need conjures up the messianic moment—at least some of the time it does.

"No More War" (Poster)
Käthe Kollwitz, 1924

Is there a dismal history to be written of embryonic political movements aborted for want of a great graphic designer? One ought to be careful about claiming too much for art, but fires die for lack of kindling. So I suspect that there may be such a history, though I'm not sure I want anyone to bother unearthing it.

Returning to the passage from *Charterhouse*, it should be pointed out that Gros sketches his caricature three days after the French have taken Milan, and the Archduke's reign is already over; rather than simply helping overturn a greedy tyrant, Gros is also doing his part in cementing French domination of the Milanese, replacing Austro-Hungarian/Spanish domination. Stendhal's infallible irony drew him to this, a fat pig of an archduke being skewered graphically by a caricaturist whose name means "big"—and who did, in fact, become "famous" as an anti-Romanticist conservative painter whose epic canvasses flattered newly minted emperors and kings (and who finally committed suicide).

It's hardly news: Politics is impure, political actors human and fallible, and the battles of opposites are never sharp edged. Twenty-first-century admirers of great political graphic design can't banish an uneasiness in appreciating design's power to catalyze change. We've seen too often how great design successfully sells monstrous lies, and we know how closely related to the whole process of selling and branding, of merchandising and commodifying, how intimately related to business, to commerce, all graphic art is. The marketplace created graphic design, its vocabulary, its ether. This is to say nothing more than that an appreciation of the progressive power of great political graphic design leads us to an appreciation of how inescapable the language of oppression and exploitation is, even in the struggle against oppres-

The Bug As Vermin
Exterminator (Magazine)
John Heartfield, 1933

sion—an appreciation shaped more elegantly by the French than by any other culture, from Stendhal through Proust through Althusser. This awareness can lead to despair, if one concludes that change is impossible, or to hope, if one concludes that every phenomenon, including language, including the language of oppression, carries within itself the seeds of its own unraveling.

So great is our knowledge, in the early years of the twenty-first century, of all that has come before us, so vast is our experience of both human success and also staggering, holocaustic failure, and so sophisticated is our understanding of how little we understand, how vaguely we understand, that a toxic cynicism pervades our spirit, shutting down our capacity for faith, for hope, for imagining change—and consequently shutting down our passion, our imagination. These posters, these works of art, have a restorative power. Each is an argument that stamps itself indelibly in on the soul of the passer-by; accepted or rejected, the argument, the claim, or demand each makes becomes a spark in the dialectical engine of consciousness, of human life. The best of these posters speak with a direct force, past all our qualifying, temporizing, even our scrupling and wisdom, to our passion, our appetite, our starved hunger for communal understanding, for collective agency, for belonging, for justice, and for change.

–Tony Kushner © 2005

Silence=Death (Poster)
Act Up, New York, 1986

Tony Kushner, born in Manhattan in July of 1956, grew up in Lake Charles, Louisiana, where his family moved after inheriting a lumber business. He earned a bachelor's degree from Columbia University and later did postgraduate work at New York University. In the early 1980s, he founded a theater group and began writing and producing plays. In the early 1990s, he scored a monster hit with the epic, seven-hour, two-part, Broadway blockbuster *Angels in America: A Gay Fantasia on National Themes*, which earned a Pulitzer Prize, two Tony Awards, two Drama Desk Awards, the Evening Standard Award, two Olivier Award Nominations, the New York Critics Circle Award, the Los Angeles Drama Critics Circle Award, and the LAMBDA Liberty Award for Drama. This groundbreaking play focuses on three households in turmoil: a gay couple, one of whom has AIDS; a Mormon man coming to terms with his sexuality; and the infamous lawyer Roy Cohn, a historical figure who died of AIDS in 1986, denying his homosexuality all the way to his deathbed. *Newsweek* wrote of *Angels in America:*

"Daring and Dazzling! The most ambitious American play of our time: an epic that ranges from earth to heaven; focuses on politics, sex and religion; transports us to Washington, the Kremlin, the South Bronx, Salt Lake City and Antarctica; deals with Jews, Mormons, WASPs, blacks; switches between realism and fantasy, from the tragedy of AIDS to the camp comedy of drag queens to the death or at least the absconding of God."

MILTON GLASER INTERVIEWED BY STEVEN HELLER

Heller: In oppressive societies, dissent is alternately called subversion, reaction, blasphemy, and is usually viewed as a criminal act. In the United States, dissent is a positive thing. Would you agree?

Glaser: It depends what the meaning of "positive" is, to paraphrase our former president. Dissent seems to have a liturgical quality, or, at least, a reference to the dogma of the church, and I think the word was used more frequently in that sense than almost any other, where there was a dissent from the agreed-upon conventions of the church by people who wanted to modify or change those conventions.

Heller: You mean the way that Martin Luther launched the Reformation when he nailed his Ninety-Five Theses to the door of the Wittenberg Church?

Glaser: Yes, among others. It seems to me that dissent disagrees with religious dogma as often as it does about political dogma. Although in both cases, they are attempts to deal with existing power.

Heller: Changing an established order is the goal of dissent. But is it done in a constructive or destructive way?

Glaser: It can be either. Dissenters usually have the idea that their dissent is an attempt to improve an existing condition. Although I suppose in the American South, when racist Southerners were demonstrating against the Civil Rights movement, from our point of view, we might say that the reaction was motivated by self-interest rather than a sense of fairness.

Heller: Were they using "dissent" as their operative term, or was it a blatant rejection of the federal government's imposition of equal rights?

NTING TIONS

Glaser: I'm not sure it's relevant whether people use the word "dissent" or not. They certainly disagreed with the government and an aspect of dissent is disagreement. We like to feel dissent is about a notion of fairness that is being violated by the existing power structure.

Heller: Is fairness the key issue?

Glaser: This notion of fairness may be intrinsic to our species. Adam Cohen in the *New York Times* ["Editorial Observer; What the Monkeys Can Teach Humans About Making America Fairer" – September 21, 2003] wrote about experiments conducted by scientists in Scandinavia with Capuchin monkeys proving that when they were all fed the same kind of food they were very cooperative and would exchange things for the food that they were given. But as soon as one member of the group was given a delicacy that was considered to be superior to what the rest were

all receiving, the monkeys went crazy. They could not stand the idea that they were not treated equally or fairly. From this, the observation was made, and apparently for the first time, that a sense of fairness is intrinsic to primates, an idea that goes beyond our individual cultures, where it sometimes exists as a precept, but actually is in the racial memory of the species. One can only assume that this structure is a way to promote the survival of the species. So fairness itself may have represented a biological device to protect the species by developing a sense of community.

Heller: But how does this unfold in the face of world behavior where we see various groups subjugate others and, thus, impose unfair conditions on the vanquished? This happens every day. Obviously, unfairness provokes dissent.

Glaser: You wouldn't need a sense of fairness if the desire for power and the instinct to kill one's enemy

ACKNOWLDGEMENTS

JESSI ARRINGTON • AMY AXLER
SIMONA BARTA • DANA BARTELT
AMIR BERBIĆ • TERRENCE BROWN
ASJA DUPANOVIĆ • EKREM DUPANOVIĆ
STEVEN HELLER • ALEXANDRA KANE
ČEDOMIR KOSTOVIĆ • DEJAN KRŠIĆ
JEE-EUN LEE • MARIJA MILJKOVIĆ
DAOUD SARHANDI • ARABA SIMPSON
STAFF OF TIPOGRAFICA MAGAZINE
SCHOOL OF VISUAL ARTS • GARTH WALKER
LAETITIA WOLFF • HELEN WU